This is a work of nonfiction. The author has written from personal experience and insight. Readers are encouraged to use their own discretion and judgment in applying the material.

ISBN: 979-8-9994246-0-0
Book design by E. J. Albert
Printed in the United States of America

First Edition

THE ABSOLUTE PATH

A Spiritual Guide to Eternal Fulfillment

—◇—

by E. J. Albert

Because after my darkest nights
You brightened up my day
And gave me all respite
When I watched you play

So here your seed grows,
I dedicate this to you—
A spirit given from a Rose...
and Rocket too!

Table of Contents

Preface

I didn't write this book as a teacher. I wrote it as someone who searched—relentlessly—for something real. Before writing this, I was an equipment operator, spending long hours alone in a box, stuck with myself. This "self" was the one I had been identified with for most of my life—a self marred by despair, resentment, and self-hatred. Many can relate. It's to them, to you, that I speak through this book.

The elements were all there: a procrastinated life, enslaved to a mediocre wage, hour after hour in a five-by-five box, while enduring the peak of my life's suffering—driven by the same desperation that had always haunted me.

Eventually, I turned inward, as if I had no choice. The suffering intensified until it gave birth to a burning need to understand—not the world, but me, at the most fundamental level. That search, and the unshakable dedication it demanded, led me deeper into something I hadn't expected: silence, presence, peace—a freedom I hadn't known was possible.

That experience came first, and I'll return to it several times in this book, from different vantage points. The writing of this book came months later— not to preach, but to share what had proven itself. And in doing so, my understanding deepened. It comes from the learned dedication, clarity, and practice from that previous experience.

If I've developed any insight since then, it's only because I've stayed close to this subject. I've studied it, returned to it, and revised this work again and again—not out of perfectionism, but out of respect for what it represents. Over the course of three years of writing this book, my understanding of that spiritual exeperience and mindfulness has grown. But it all began with something simple: the end of suffering, and the recognition of something in me that didn't need fixing. And from that space, something new emerged—the ability to observe, and to stay close to the truth of all things.

This is not a book about manifestation. It won't hand you everything you desire. What it offers instead is a path to uncover the life that's always been here—free, still, undivided. If there's anything I can promise, it's that these steps worked for me. They led me beyond striving, beyond even the need to practice, into a fulfillment that requires no maintenance.

You might call it mindfulness, but it goes further. This book is for those ready to walk a path deep into spirit—into knowing themselves beyond what's familiar. Into the kind of peace that remains. It just takes a leap.

"A little whim of will to be free gallantly contending with the universe of chemistry."

— Ralph Waldo Emerson,
The Conduct of Life

INTRODUCTION

Not long ago, during a transitional period in my life, chance led me to a job at a notable, secluded horse ranch. After some consideration, I accepted—my life had generally been in limbo up to that point, so why say no? Plus, it was free housing. The place was beautiful, the people were great, and I didn't mind spending days caring for horses and weed whacking. It was a peaceful time, mostly, and even the little bit of horse training I picked up taught me a few valuable lessons about myself.

One day, I faced a simple problem. I was tasked to unknot the (very) tangled mane of a filly, who had been out to pasture for a few weeks. Despite spraying endless detangler and fervent brushing, tugging, and pulling, the thick mane remained a mess on this indifferent horse. Someone, I think the farrier, suggested I just cut out the knots, but I couldn't give up. For around an hour, I struggled and made no progress; in fact, it may have even worsened. It's embarrassing, but I've never claimed to be the sharpest tool in the shed.

Finally, the ranch manager—who was also an expert horse trainer—stepped in to show me how it's done. It was something to behold. He simply took the mane, lightly fluffed it out, and let the hair fall as it may, only pulling when needed with no unnecessary force. Soon everything was detangled and even, and the task was done. As the boss walked away, and for some time after, I considered a lesson in his method.

What doesn't bend snaps to unkown force. What doesn't move gets left behind. There is a need in just about all of us to always be right; a drive to fortify ourselves in our own, and everybody else's, mind. This rightness consistently gets us into trouble, creating resistance and resentment within ourselves and in personal relationships, and at times hindering the possibilities of success, so that all can be as you want it to be.

We expect every expectation to be met and fortified, otherwise, we may not be important. We might even augment our expectations to better shape our surroundings, crafting a more valuable personality. Maybe we're happy, or maybe not; it depends on whether anything gets in the way and irritates our new and improved self.

Like a marionette, your strings get pulled by problem-perpetuating thoughts, by anxiety, guilt, or the relentless tide of negative emotion, from being motivated to unmotivated. Is it possible that most of the stress you experience isn't an unchangeable part of you, but a shadow cast by the belief that you are your thoughts and emotions? Too often, we identify ourselves with our struggles, some even saying self-defeating phrases like, "*I am insecure*" or "*I am angry.*" This belief traps us in endless manipulation, where we try to control our surroundings in a desperate attempt to avoid discomfort. The mind has its limitations, but within all of us there is an inkling of limitlessness.

But what if you gave up that control? The expectations? Those feelings that make you...you? What would be left? Perhaps if all the apprehension, negativity, and problems could be allowed to fall where they may, maybe something deeper, some lost meaning—that thing people like to talk and write about vaguely when reaching deep—would reveal itself to us.

Consider these two alternatives for a moment: first, that you are your thoughts, shaped entirely by the conditions that led to them, with awareness reduced to a blank, passive state. It doesn't exist. Thoughts and actions simply move, unnoticed, without attention placed on them. Like what you might imagine the apex of a robot to be, one day. There's something strange and dark in this; notice how difficult it is even to imagine. Take your time. Really try to have some sense of zero awareness.

Now shift your focus. Imagine, instead, that you're not at the mercy of your thoughts, but simply observing. Try to feel pure awareness, this time thoughtless, yet alert as if you're operating without surface thinking. Does this feel more natural? At least, plausible? This is the difference between machine and human—this is conscious awareness.

When you question your actions, when you long for something greater, who is it that speaks from within? That quiet voice seems to come from somewhere deeper, closer to that observer—the true self. The hero of your story. Steadfast and reliable, always ready to rise above the illusions of the thoughts, of ego.

In contrast, the ego—cut off from spirit—may be the villain. It's driven by fear, clouded by judgment and expectation, blinding us from the self we seek. It convinces us that we're nothing more than its impulses. But still, it feels as though there is always something inside, beyond the surface, waiting, watching, ready to return you to a lost sense of wholeness.

This eternal struggle, known as duality, is the battleground where your absolute consciousness meets the conditioned mind. To break free from the chains of conditioning, we must clear the mental obstacles and reconnect with consciousness unobscured by the limitations of personhood. Only then can we embrace the state of non-duality—true Absolution.

Why do we treat our negative emotions as separate entities, yet allow them to define us? This paradox reveals a simple truth: our emotional turbulence stems from an internal distortion—a lower self that seeks control and validation rather than embracing life as it is. In this journey of self-discovery, we strive to integrate ego into spirit, learning to observe rather than be consumed by this mistaken identity. By letting go of being right and what we cannot control, and all the regret thereafter, we begin to detach from the ego and move toward our true essence.

While we each have different propensities, emotional tendencies, and sensitivities, to suggest that these conditions forever bind us is to deny the extraordinary potential within us. It's true that for many, medication or therapy may help find balance, but it's also true that countless individuals have shifted their mental and emotional states through inner work, mindfulness, and surrender. The idea that we're incapable of true, lasting transformation denies the vast human capacity for change.

The fact that transformation is possible—seen time and time again, and often in cases where external circumstances suggest otherwise—shows that the mind is not an unchangeable machine. To rely solely on the idea that "this is the way we are, and it cannot change" is a limited perspective. This is the despairing ego accepting its desperation. By opening ourselves up to the possibility of growth, we tap into the malleability of both mind and body, a truth that outshines the many deterministic views of human biology.

Much of this modern determinism is merely karma without Buddha's path, Emerson's fate without the Oversoul, a children's story without the moral lesson, and so on. The discoveries in science about *what* makes us determined are exceptionally valuable, but the philosophical attitude shouldn't be treated as if it were original. It isn't to know that things are determined that is the great discovery; it is to accept this as *yourself* without question (whether knowledgeable of the fact or not), that has been pointed out time and again, by the holiest and most influential of thinkers, as the greatest ignorance.

It isn't to say that strict determinism doesn't underpin exactly how spirituality suggests we should treat others and ourselves; after all, isn't the greatest prudence to treat others as ourselves, as if all else were a product of a determined universe outside our control? So, following either spirituality's or scientific logic, there seems to be either a universal self or no self at all—and it also seems there is little, perhaps no, difference between the two. I'm amongst those who push for the universal self, and I call this the Absolute (sometimes *spirit* or *higher self*, amongst others). This is because I promote allowing awareness to stand alone, removing the ego completely, and seeing what happens. It's not only about knowing things are determined and thinking about people in this manner, but about separating yourself from what is determined, to enact a change in consciousness, and in becoming consciousness itself. In becoming one with consciousness, a truth emerges: consciousness is the prerequisite to life, not the outcome.

To practice mindfulness and spirituality is to acknowledge that our current mental or emotional state does not bind us, nor does our chemical makeup imprison us. We are something deeper—something that, when found, *can* create change, heal, and transform, even when society says otherwise. The outliers, the individuals who have transcended their limitations, remind us that this potential exists within all of us.

Heart Over Matter

Too many of us despair in an overactive, negative mind, convinced that transformation is beyond our reach. Settling into a fear-induced comfort, we need force and manipulation for upkeep. We spend our energy fighting the symptoms using the same thing that creates them, overlooking the root cause, unable to see beyond the clouds of perceived problems.

The issue has hardly ever been the situations life brings to us, which might be better seen as just challenges or tasks. Instead, it's the negative and repetitive thoughts and words that ensue—turning neutral events into problems and objects of exaggerated fear through compulsive repetition—along with unchecked habitual negative emotions. The more we indulge in these patterns, the more entrenched they become, creating a self that is stuck in suffering.

The mind, misused for impractical purposes, inevitably fails to meet the vast array of personal expectations set before it. This failure leads us to try to force our surroundings and relationships into meeting these mentally dogmatic expectations. Caught in the grip of fixation on endless conceived comforts and wants, we face endless self-judgments and questions, whether from the past or the anticipation of the future. Misery in its various forms binds us in an ongoing cycle, locking us in a perpetual oscillation between hope and dread, believing there is no end.

Instead, learn to end constant rumination and live seated at the heart, where the breath lies to rest and the one unchanging consciousness resides. Let everything take its course. This practice is often referred to as presence—living in the moment, unattached to outcomes, focused, and surrendering to an energy within. Cease all fear driven by endless conceptualizing and the relentless crafting of stories. Prioritize the aspects of your life that deserve your attention now and make this your new standard.

When we begin to clear our mind and quiet the incessant noise, while existing firmly at the heart, our choices in life become markedly clearer. The fog of overthinking dissipates, allowing paths and decisions that align more closely with our true selves. This newfound clarity enables us to make decisions from a place of calmness and confidence, rather than regret and confusion. We begin to see options and opportunities that were previously obscured by our mental clutter, bringing with them a more intentional and authentic life.

Interested in *Manifestation?*

Living with presence naturally leads to manifestation, though your idea of manifestation might change once you enter into a more spiritual or mindful way of being. The formula is not a secret one—replace mental fear (self-judgment, anticipation) with inner inspiration to free up your life. There's no need to seek mysterious powers; when the need for useless thoughts and negative emotions dissipates, dwelling and clinging do too, making life naturally easier. Remember, there is only failure in regret. By eliminating regret, you stack the deck in your favor because you can only lose what *feels* lost.

The same applies to attracting favorable circumstances. If you live from a place of inner peace and have overcome your inner demons, people and situations will naturally turn in your favor. Who doesn't want to associate with someone who discovered the key to everlasting joy? And what situation isn't benefited by an inspired attitude and singular focus? My advice on manifestation is this: let go of results—past and future, positive and negative—while lightly holding onto your creative inspiration and what brings you the most joy. Make the work itself the goal. Be like the professional quarterback or pitcher: whether your last play was great or terrible, move on to the next with a consistent and focused attitude. The same can be said for the nurse or salesman; previous experience needs to be set aside for the duty to be fulfilled to perfection. As it is, I'm not offering a course on manifestation; this is, at its core, a spirituality-based experience, rooted in my understanding—an end to suffering. Still, there are a few outstanding differences in the teachings, but manifestation practices will always be met by a wall of wanting that should eventually be dropped (if true transcendence is desired).

This book provides a step-by-step guide to overcoming states of dwelling, clinging, and negative mind chatter, and, most importantly, to embracing inner peace. The method I present is one I discovered while eliminating my poor mental habits; through natural progression and inspiration, I achieved complete inner stillness in less than two months. I now outline how this occurred, and the stages of this transformation, including specific mindsets and practical approaches that will benefit anyone seeking guidance toward a more direct and fulfilling path.

My Path and Relationships

About a year into working at the horse stables, I extended my reach for something a bit too out of reach and fell deeply in love. Not long after, she became pregnant with our child. The surrounding circumstances weren't ideal, to put it lightly, and I won't delve into specifics; let's just say I wasn't a hero in this story. Eventually, I had to leave my comfortable life behind, finding myself in a new job and a whole new reality. This shift brought with it a whirlwind of discomfort, and through these storms, I was forced to confront myself in ways I had never faced before. It was during these trials that I stumbled upon what some might call an awakening—a realization that I'm not just my mind but the observer of it, searching for an end to my cycle of suffering. Here's how it unfolded:

From the beginning, our relationship was on shaky ground, and things got worse during the pregnancy. I was consistently overwhelmed by anger, sadness, and confusion, with brief moments of motivation that quickly fizzled out into apathy. It felt like I was on a rollercoaster, blindfolded and strapped in tight, with no indication when the next twist, turn, drop, or end would hit. I was only afforded a few hours of sleep most nights during this dark period of my life.

The kind of sleep where upon waking, I would find myself absorbed in the same argument I was in—with an imaginary other—through all hours of the previous day and while trying to fall asleep. It was as if I had been talking in my sleep, in the same fashion as if I were awake, with no break. There was no dreaming or respite of slumber—only endless diatribes and mental repetition of the recent failures. In one month, I lost thirty pounds—turns out, a poor relationship is a great way to lose your appetite, where a bag of candy during lunch at an unfocused job was the total of my daily diet. It was imagination at its cruelest, a cage. If the mind were deemed a slave master, then the mind entrenched in this sort of self-abuse is an abusive master indeed.

Every conversation in our relationship inevitably turned into an argument. One day, after a particularly heated exchange, I found myself alone in the dark, broken down into tears, screaming continuously in my head like a frightened child: "I don't want to fight anymore!" That breakdown led to something I can only describe as a sudden visceral awakening, or *satori*. The next morning, the things that had been eating away at me just...stopped. I felt lighter, as if a mountain of burden had been lifted away. This inexplicable sense of peace lasted for a while, and I clung to it, hoping it would continue forever. I even tried to dissect the experience for a secret formula to keep it going. But back then, I had no insight into anything considered "mindful." From what I gather now, a satori is an intuitive, brief period of profound mindfulness, although it may vary greatly in length.

But as much as I wished it could last forever, the peace of my satori lasted only a week. My partner noticed the change in me, and we decided to have a day together. When you become more present, people naturally gravitate toward you. Despite my reservations about the timing, I agreed to it. Initially, everything went smoothly—we had lunch, laughed, and shared encouraging smiles. But as the day wore on, old habits resurfaced, shattering the tranquility of my satori. My ego crept back in, undoing the peace I had found.

This part of my story may seem insignificant, but it illustrates the profound impact that suffering can have on us unconsciously. Deep down, I was exhausted by the constant conflict, like a child desperate for peace between arguing parents. Driven to my limit, I surrendered completely, letting go of the personal stakes I had been clinging to. This type of surrender has happened to countless others in similar and worse circumstances throughout history. Whether this occurs due to an internal panic button, or an unconscious or spiritual mutiny, I don't know. But it does happen, and it deserves more attention.

After some time apart, we moved back in together, now with a child. She was hopeful we could work, but I knew there was still shakiness to the situation. Unfortunately, old insecurities resurfaced, casting a shadow over our relationship. Healing takes time—more than we would like to admit—and it's hard to acknowledge this, especially to someone else. The lesson here can be to take the breaks when needed and let the wounds heal, but I know this is easier said than done. Eventually, she moved out again. This time, losing my daughter's consistent presence in my life was the driving factor that motivated me to do better. But I didn't have another satori.

I had been searching for answers before, but now I was on a deeper quest. And suddenly, I came across an answer that struck a chord: *nobody* has the right to your emotions. In other words, my happiness shouldn't depend on someone else or their emotional state. I'm sure I had heard this before, but everyone's timing and needed message is different (though this lesson seems to be a popular starting point). I was then ready to absorb it, and it shifted my perspective.

I realized my insecurities were rooted in my attachment to outside sources, in fear of loss, and in my tendency to let my emotional state be dictated by things outside my control, particularly another person.

Before, I was obsessed with figuring out how to make someone stay connected to me, not understanding that joy comes from within. Instead of trying to manipulate emotions to achieve a specific outcome, I learned to let go of that outcome, as well as any anticipation or guilt associated with it. This shift was significant—for the first time in my life, I felt like I had direct control over my mental focus. Before then, it felt like I was a slave to my emotions and thoughts. But now, I discovered that my mind was not the ultimate authority, and that letting go was possible, because somehow, I *was* letting go. This revelation brought about the most change and power to constructively move forward. *I now had a choice.*

That marked the beginning of my mindfulness journey. As I grew stronger philosophically and explored various techniques, I delved deeper inward, day after day, moment after moment, prioritizing practice and focus above all else. Over time, the practice became easier, so easy that not practicing felt unnatural. My thoughts seemed to need persuading to enter. Seconds began to feel like minutes, and minutes like hours; this was perfectly fine by me. It was no longer as if I were just part of nature and the world; instead, the world was there for me to observe and absorb. Then one day, I experienced something I never thought possible—I ceased thinking effortlessly and lived in a state of peace and pure objectivity. There were no more thoughts to be noticed as they faded away, and there were no more emotional experiences outside necessity. I still participated in all the same activities and spoke when needed, but I had become impenetrable and independent.

In a sense, a relationship was my catalyst, so I won't deny the significant influence it holds in life. My approach might seem like I erased the relationship from my mind, but it wasn't that I didn't want a relationship; rather, it was my main source of dwelling, and I decided it should only exist in the moment. I couldn't allow myself to be drawn into any familiar darkness if it presented itself. I had to become more present.

I began to see most of my negative thought patterns had taken root in the relationship. Since I didn't want to be led down any old paths, I did my best to always maintain a sense of inner appreciation, while surrendering to my heart during emotional lows, and all while observing my mind and surroundings without thoughts or labels.

As you progress, you might notice certain individuals—unconsciously caught in their patterns—trying to draw you into emotional turmoil. Not just in intimate relationships but in all interactions. You will be tested around every corner; it's simply the nature of the world and all the coinciding stories. Every thought and action has its compensation, whether it's dealing with a dramatic person or a simple instance of intertwining lives, and every choice you make.

When these challenges arise, practice staying rooted in the moment. Sit with any discomfort. Let the urge to weave narratives or fixate on the details go. This technique will be explored more deeply in Step two on surrender.

I'll note that this doesn't mean you should be cold or indifferent to your partner or anyone. On the contrary, this practice will create a resounding opposite effect; your heart will naturally open with little effort. You will see the power of the space you give not just in your mind, but in your relationships as well. There will be room to breathe, and an atmosphere that allows for complete authenticity for everyone involved. You're not separating yourself; you're creating unity by removing the separate, obstructive self.

I also encourage not trying to persuade your partner into becoming mor spiritually conscious. It's a beautiful thing if you can walk the path together—

supporting each other through any lapse and engaging in meaningful meditative practices. However, if they're not on the same page, it's important to respect that boundary.

Let your practice be sacred. If someone becomes curious, feel free to share your experiences, but let them discover their way. Avoid forcing your practice on them, as coercion is contrary to the spirit of mindfulness. If you want, allow the relationship be your inspiration, but not your soapbox. Focus on establishing *your* inner peace. Let that light illuminate the lives around you, and they will not need to be convinced of anything.

If you seek clarity of mind, there must no longer be places in which it dwells. Let things to be as they are. If you're in an agonizing relationship that's struggling to get sorted out, you can make mistakes without apologizing for every minor error or judging yourself too harshly. It's not bad to express regret, but don't obsess over how others feel; ultimately, they are responsible for their own emotions. It is up to you to get back to yours and allow yourself to be that light. You can offer support and love to others, but it is crucial to prioritize your inner state. The best way to help is through an unmovable, joyful way of being that they can aspire to. There may be a sense of arrogance to this when you practice at first, and that's fine. Know that selfishness takes and expects from others; self-love is concerned with inner peace, which takes no part in acts of selfishness.

This approach also involves honesty. If you're choosing not to engage with someone else's negativity, you can't expect them to absorb yours. Part of mental clarity involves freeing yourself from being easily offended and seeking answers or validation externally. While it might seem harsh, minimizing dependence on relationships is essential. Over-reliance on others to enhance your life can create undue pressure and strain, both on yourself and your relationships. The more complete you feel within, the more fully you can show up for others.

If it isn't clear, I'm not advocating anything unconventional regarding monogamy or commitment, which I personally value. Instead, I want to highlight how dependency can strain both individual lives and relationships. Usual relationships, by their nature, involve a deep level of attachment and the interplay of two egos. When one person becomes unhappy and the other follows, compounding the disconnect, often spiraling into a cycle of mutual unhappiness. Breaking this cycle can be transformative, and it starts with eliminating roles centered on emotional servitude. This book aims to provide practical steps for doing so without succumbing to arrogance, personal vendettas, or laziness. While trying not to be overly philosophical, the guidance here is designed to help anyone navigating these challenges.

There is no need to expect the perfect partner, manipulate situations to work to your advantage, or create comfortable scenarios at the expense of a loved one. This will never work, it will always just be work— the kind of work that leads to resentment. Our minds are not built for such tasks; they lead to perpetual stress and unreasonable expectations. Learn to exist in the moment without grasping or manipulating. When you let go of these burdens, all that remains is the weightlessness of mutual love.

Presence, Warnings, and Discipline.

Living in the present means that a problem presents itself once. Presence not only augments a difficulty in life but will usually be the solution. When you live bound by the notion of past and future—constantly projecting into a moment that doesn't exist—you give them more importance than the present moment, fueling regret and unnecessary anticipation.

Notice how, during moments of great joy or deep flow, time seems to be irrelevant? That's because it is. Deep down, you recognize this state as your true essence. The desire to be fully in the moment and fulfilled is a natural goal; yet, it's the mind's misuse in pursuing this goal that leads to suffering. Achieving a consistent flow state and living each moment in joyful peace is possible—it requires recognizing your true essence and using the mind as the tool it was meant to be, not the master of your experiences.

The use of the mind leads to what are spiritually referred to as 'samskaras'—the events from our past that shape our habitual reactions. It's this negative conditioning that we must root out by living in the present, through consistent practice that becomes easier over time. These ingrained patterns can cloud your clarity and hinder your ability to live a joyfully balanced, unconditional life.

Let go of past burdens and let the future unfold naturally; it will not harm you. There is liberation in breaking these habits. You must drop the notion of being a great problem solver by taking everything that has happened or been done to you personally. This mindset has only created unnecessary problems through senseless dwelling.

Whenever in doubt, take a deep, slow breath—*and accept the moment.* Embrace yielding, never forceful; this should be the cornerstone of your approach. Allow everything to exist as it is, free from the constraints of time, and only the things that truly deserve your attention will remain. This is to encourage the highest form of confidence: if you give everything its rightful place, anguish will diminish. Navigate through life's challenges by releasing mental clutter and permitting the present awareness to guide you. Surrender to the moment and anchor yourself in the heart.

In this style of acceptance, it should be regarded as letting go of the need to always be right. Acceptance is the approach to kickstarting progress, because, after all, you cannot progress if your ego is constantly resisting to maintain itself. Acceptance isn't creating a passive ego; it's dropping the ego's insatiable, exaggerated desire for rightness. And remember, it isn't just the need to be right in explicit thinking, but also in the ego's constant implicit intention; so, it must be dealt with the opposite intention—acceptance, letting go.

You're here to eliminate despair and end mental noise. I don't recommend power seeking or some great spiritual attainment as your primary motivation. Those accomplishments may naturally occur, but they should not arise from self-serving desires. Let the cessation of grasping and a mind that rests peacefully be your motivation instead. This approach offers a more profound inspiration than a sense of attainment ever could.

Seeking and obtaining are the mind's way of functioning and may seem satisfying, but they often become obstacles. Our goal is to remove these blockages to achieve clarity and spiritual freedom. Attainment will follow naturally from your practice, not from a desperate 'wanting.' I say this because in my personal journey, I never considered enlightenment as a goal or even as a possibility. I was suffering, so I just stuck to what seemed to help, moment after moment, and it worked for me, so that is my advice and my practice.

When it comes to mysticism—things such as astrology, witchcraft, fortune-telling, or mind-reading—I suggest letting these notions as aspects of spirituality go (to each their own, only seeing the difference). If spirituality is about transcending the personality into a singular, focused, non-dual state, then how can following beliefs and practices that emphasize personality be recommended? Whether any of it is real or not doesn't matter. To look to stars lightyears apart from each other as a sign of what makes up your personality and who best suits it, or learning a secret spell to manipulate people and things in your favor, or to see into a future that should be let go, if anything, are anti-spiritual by nature, either in conceptual desire or in the belief it holds substance to your true being.

It's one thing to be inspired by a spiritual experience, but in this, too, don't let it carry you away. It's not uncommon to encounter moments that feel supernatural or life-altering, but becoming fixated on such experiences can be a trap. This obsession, much like other mental distractions, will hinder your progress. Not only can it lead to stagnation, but the process itself—when overemphasized or romanticized—can fuel a sense of grandiosity, inflating the ego under the guise of spiritual development. In extreme cases, this can lead to crazed fanaticism or destructive behaviors.

While the idea that you are not your mind but something more akin to pure energy may seem fantastical, it emerges from rational self-examination, mental resignation, and a willingness to self-test through experience. The capacity for flexible reasoning should never be traded for fantasies about personal spiritual experiences; allow these experiences their due sacredness. Remember, the mind mainly operates beyond what surface thinking fully comprehends. To assume that an experience or vivid vision has no connection to the brain's deeper processes is misguided, even if the experience feels, and by all accounts is, undeniably extraordinary. This is the one caution that must be heeded in spiritual practice: while spiritual experiences can be profound, becoming attached to them or allowing them to fuel a sense of self-importance can derail your journey toward true understanding and balance.

Before moving on, it's essential to make a clear distinction: awakening is not enlightenment. Awakening is the realization that you're not the ego, that your thoughts are not your true self. But this recognition alone is not the end of the full spiritual path; it's where the practice begins. Being fully identified with the ego is closer to awakening than awakening is to enlightenment, though the path from that realization to its completion cannot be denied.

One of the most common mistakes among spiritual seekers is to stop at this early stage, where they pause the mind for periods with consistent casual confidence, believing they have reached the summit. While recognition is essential, enlightenment is not merely a belief or a commitment to the idea that "I'm not the ego." It's the completed transformation. It's no longer thinking at all, not even about being enlightened. Thoughts must be summoned, as if recalling a lost art. It's a knowing beyond belief, where spiritual rapture has been integrated into sustained bliss.

This misunderstanding is where the latent ego often hides. It convinces the seeker they have arrived, then inflates itself with subtle pride. Plato expresses a similar dynamic in *The Republic,* describing those who believe they've reached the height of understanding, though they've only perceived shadows cast by firelight. Even if they come to recognize they've only been watching shadows, committed to their limited experience, they may never walk beyond the cave, never to witness the blinding truth that waits outside.

You can often spot this confusion when someone dismisses long-standing spiritual teachings—sometimes even critiquing the Buddha himself—claiming "that teacher still speaks as ego," or rejecting practices like breathwork or surrender as unnecessary. These are not signs of depth, but of self-aggrandizement. They fail to see where the sages are speaking from, simply because the sage understands the whole arc of the process. Returning to Plato's allegory (though I might be stretching it thin), it's like the one who comes back to the cave to describe what he has seen, only to be mocked by those who cannot yet understand. Enlightenment, as pointed out by the greatest traditions, doesn't rest in awakening alone. It stands beyond it—from the quiet, humbling work of transmuting the ego's residue, until every trace dissolves.

Persevere. Continue your efforts, and everything will come together. The task may seem daunting at times, and you might feel like giving up. There may come times of desperation or depression, anger or angst, where results seem few and far between. Hold onto the reins firmly, whether you fall off the moment you mount or even after you feel secure, get back on. Enjoy the journey, trusting that the practice will bear fruit and wounds will heal. With practice, you will master how to steer, reverse, accelerate, and decelerate as needed in the moment. In due course, you can use your senses and intuition effortlessly, becoming one with who you are.

This book outlines clear steps: know the ego, go within, observe, and confirm who you truly are. It includes meditations designed to foster growth. These are simple, time-tested approaches. The sequence and methods I present are those I naturally discovered and used myself, and I believe they can be effective for anyone. This book answers the frequently asked but often unaddressed spiritual question, 'But what do I do?' It provides a straightforward discipline, leaving no room for confusion or ambiguous responses.

It's important to understand that the practice builds cumulatively. Each step should build upon the next, rather than being treated as a separate lesson. Also, the philosophical aspects are just as important as the practices, in that they help the path become more visible and promote behavior to keep you on that path, but always remember that it's up to you to live by *your* chosen principles. As you master each step, the process will require less effort and flow more naturally. Don't advance to the next step until you have consistently practiced the current one and are confident in your understanding. This ensures a solid foundation for your spiritual journey.

Meditation

At the end of each step, I will provide a brief recap of the practice, along with a corresponding daily meditation. Meditation is an excellent tool for nurturing presence, offering a space to practice mindfulness in a focused and direct manner, and helping to ease into a state of readiness. Primarily, I view meditation as a way to either reclaim a sense of space, perhaps lost, or to amplify your progress and set a strong tone for the rest of your day. It can also serve as a practice ground for specific presence techniques aimed at overall improvement. While meditation can be a valuable tool for relaxation, in this context, we utilize it as a catalyst for growth.

The meditations I suggest are designed to help promote precision and facilitate a smooth transition to the next step. They are meant to be less demanding than the practices outlined in the steps, ensuring they don't feel burdensome while remaining crucial for progress. If there is any particular style of meditation that resonates with you, feel free to incorporate it. Aim for ten to thirty minutes per session, always embracing the core principles of the practice. Remember to take your time in between the words, embracing silence and space. Regardless of the meditation style, *always seek a deeper internal connection.*

I have personally found it beneficial to meditate during breaks at work—typically three sessions of five to ten minutes each in my car, plus one twenty-minute session at home. This routine made for what I consider a near-perfect day, though not every day will be like this. For me, these meditations often served as a way to ease into a more solid foundation in spirituality, until I reached my next meditation, and then I would repeat. Find what works best for you. A single quality meditation session each day can be beneficial, but striving for more frequent practice can further enhance consistency.

I'm also among those who believe that meditation benefits from intentional structure—that is, having planned or preferred times dedicated to practice. Some suggest that meditation should come naturally and spontaneously, as if effort or scheduling contradicts spiritual authenticity. But this misinterprets the concept of "letting go." Letting go, or letting things unfold naturally, refers primarily to the inner process of release in thought and emotion, achieved through consistent, moment-to-moment mindfulness, rather than the absence of structure. Many respected spiritual teachers have cautioned against this view, noting that it can signal a lack of devotion or seriousness. Setting aside time to sit and deepen your scope is not only beneficial—it's an act and proof of discipline and commitment to your well-being.

To prevail in both practice and meditation, dedication and discipline are essential. Strive to improve each day, surpassing your efforts from the day before. Commit to this discipline, creating healthier mental habits, and taking your well-being seriously. There may be times you need to sternly remind yourself you're invested spiritually and that there is no putting it off for later—there is only this moment. Embrace the process and find joy in this work. It will soon become the most rewarding and significant work you have ever undertaken.

— STEP ONE —

KNOW THE EGO

AND THE MENTAL TIME PARADOX

To turn the mind inward on itself is to chase the ultimate knowledge: to know who you are. Find a resting resolution with every thought that forms in your mind. Rather than dissecting your looming questions into parts, answer with an increasing sense of mental release, and find reality through self-expansion. Go the other way. It serves us well to question things and grow in deeper understanding, and will work well again, but the one answer does not lie in fragmentation—it's found in returning to wholeness. When you reach the end of all this, what is discovered is perfection, boundlessness, and a reality without beginning or end. When desire and attachment are finally completely relinquished, a single truth remains: the Absolute.

To cultivate the land, first clear it of the troubling sticks and boulders and enrich the soil. The deeper you dig, the cleaner the foundation, making everything else easier. The objective is to become completely aware of our thinking, sharpening the mind as a tool for recognizing itself—like preparing the blade that breaks the ground. Just as a well-prepared field makes for a good harvest, a well-observed mind lays the groundwork for inner peace and clarity.

What you do is continuously observe your ego, turning your attention inward and waiting for your thoughts to arise. The practice can look like this: a thought appears and fades, and then you might internally acknowledge it (best to keep responses in your mind), noting, "*That was my ego.*" You can take it further with an affirmation like, "*I'm not my mind. I don't judge or compulsively project myself,*" or "*I allow, I flow, and I'm grateful.*" Customize your responses to resonate with you, or simply note the thought without any additional commentary—the key is to continuously recognize that you are not your thoughts. This practice helps break the habit of identifying with the mind and builds a habit of objectivity. After acknowledging a thought, patiently wait for the next one, watching with a sense of focus and patience.

In this, you're almost physically observing your mind. Often, people don't take this lesson literally enough; they become lost in spiritual terminology. You're lightly watching and scanning the source from which thoughts emerge—somewhere inside your head, or where it seems to be—and waiting for the next thought to arise. In a way, you're actively trying to predict your next thought; by simply waiting for the answer (and watching the mind), thoughts naturally pause for a while. This gap is where the impact lies. Think of it as a mechanism to create a space between thinking, while demonstrating that you exist independently of your ego through awareness.

This technique closely parallels the psychological method of *paradoxical intention*, popularized by Dr. Viktor Frankl. His work, *Man's Search for Meaning,* where he depicts his life, struggles, and transcendence during his time in Nazi concentration camps, also accompanied by his logotherapy style, I suggest everyone should read, as soon as possible. The idea is to focus on the very thing you wish to stop—inviting it rather than resisting it. A simple and common application of this technique is in treating insomnia; instead of struggling to fall asleep, one might deliberately try to stay awake, which paradoxically relaxes the mind and allows sleep to come naturally. Here, we take a similar approach with thoughts: instead of resisting them, we observe them with a questioning attitude. We wait and expect an answer as to what our next thought will be, allowing thoughts to arise as they will, but in doing so, we create subtle pauses between them. By gently extending these gaps with patience, we begin to loosen the mind's habitual grip and move toward a state of presence.

Believe you're not your mind until it becomes an undeniable truth. When pointing out thoughts, understand that they are not you, but a creation of conditioning. So, find the answers while cultivating a generalized attitude, recognize the connections between emotions and thoughts, and their opposing thoughts, but always distinguish that this is not you. Within the pause of mental activity that follows this recognition, allow the real you to emerge and expand.

This practice forms the foundation of our overall approach because it provides the most direct means to pause mental activity. In the subsequent steps, we will discuss surrender and observation, natural follow-ups to this step. Mastering this initial practice will make those next steps more accessible and effective in your journey, offering a straightforward method to redirect your focus inward, toward the workings of the mind.

Gratitude, Indifference

As you enhance your awareness and eliminate negative conditioning, you will naturally gravitate toward more positive human qualities that are closer to your heart. Alongside accepting everything as it is, grow the virtue of *gratitude*, a powerful emotional healer that has been used for millennia. The ego thrives on a need to feel superior, so it shouldn't be difficult to see how embracing gratitude can be transformative. Be grateful not only for the simple ability to breathe and live but also for every person and event that has contributed to your life's journey.

This can be especially helpful if you are struggling with general emotional control. Whenever possible, allow a gentle sense of appreciation to emanate from within, establishing this as your emotional baseline. This is closely tied to your inner light, which will also be explored more in the next steps. However, beginning to nurture this peaceful feeling now has its benefits. Let gratitude melt into all action, and virtue will grow and sustain without the need of contemplation.

If you struggle at all or need a simple state of mind to help with this practice in Step One specifically, I also suggest *indifference*. Different from appreciation, which is an emotional state of being at ease, indifference applies explicitly to managing your thoughts and curtailing negative reactions. Envision what indifference is like and let that be the attitude toward the majority, if not all, of your thoughts. Evoke this especially in times when your mind wants to grasp onto someone else's emotions toward you or during periods of self-judgment. It doesn't require remarks or thoughts like "whatever, leave me alone," it's more aligned with space and allowing things to be. It may feel uncomfortable at first, as if you're being uncaring or even rude, but this is in your head. It's beneficial for all when done in earnest and with an open heart, and it will quickly become apparent if you pay attention.

You're generally trying to think less, and the less power a negative thought has over you, the better. Consciously shifting your attitude when staying off a sudden hurtful idea, whether toward another or yourself, is only an attempt to keep negative emotions from carrying you downstream. You're trying to gain control and become mentally stronger, and a generalized, nonchalant view of mental talk can play a key role. I say this again as a style of clearing thoughts, specifically, attempting to get ahead of any negative streams of thinking. You shouldn't try to repress any emotion—they should be felt and accepted without the story. This will be the topic in the next step.

It's also important to note, again, that this indifference is directed toward thoughts and perceived problems, rather than toward life itself. It also works best if coupled with appreciation. If practicing this technique leads to building resentment toward someone, you're probably misapplying it and should explore healthy communication instead.

Distractions

It could be necessary to minimize external distractions to better focus on the practice (and other important tasks). These distractions do more than just divert your attention—they prevent you from fully realizing the potential of these steps. By distractions, I mean any habitual activity you engage in to avoid doing something you know you should be doing, such as using your cell phone, watching TV, or aimlessly opening the refrigerator. For example, if you find yourself reaching for your phone instead of meditating, it's a sign that some work needs to be done.

Although initially challenging, actively resisting these distractions will lead to progress. Each time a distraction arises, consciously choose to say no, let it go, and refocus. This isn't creating a paradox, as discussed in paradoxical intention, because we're simply curtailing a habitual action by not doing it and accepting the slight mental strain. That being said, we can use the opportunity to pause the mind through that technique while doing so. Putting this effort forth will become easier and yield obvious benefits. Remember, every temptation resisted is an embracing of real meaning, a step closer to your authentic self.

For the remainder of this step, we will focus on what I see as the primary facets of the ego, in helping grow stronger in this practice and spiritually. I encourage you to analyze yourself to whatever extent you find necessary, but also to keep it simple. It's easy to get lost in over analysis and psychological digging. So, understand what makes you tick, but remember to strive to return to the pause in the mind, and don't forget that you cannot fully trust the mind.

If you're unsure about what the ego is exactly, understand that it shows whenever your mind uses you, rather than you using your mind. The ego is the aspect of your mind with which you've mistakenly identified, obscuring your true self. It harnesses the fight-or-flight response for conceptual rather than just real dangers, creating unnecessary fear. It's an exaggerated reality. It operates through endless, repetitive, and futile thoughts that distract you. The ego is busy solving personal problems of its own making, rather than facing life's challenges with grace. It feels sadness and anger when its conditions aren't met, and in turn, it engages in control and manipulation. The ego dwells on things, clings to them, and exists in conceptual time—it pulls you into the past or future, causing you to miss the one fluid moment and eventually leading to feelings of guilt and regret. It insists on being right at all costs, often at the expense of others, and is quick to judge.

The Judgment Parameter

All is subject to karma, or cause and effect, and all effects have their compensations, and for a living thing to mediate its compensatory existence, it must make judgments. No matter the nature of the entanglement, whether it's mild or deeply detrimental, the mind is always subject to what can be called the *judgment parameter*. This core function, over time, constructs the ego in humans, which then becomes one's sense of personhood.

Judgment is the brain's primary purpose, what it's designed to do—sense, attend, judge—and then we get beliefs and expectations. The malfunctions we experience stem from the poorly habituated tendencies in conceptual expectations—on fathomed circumstances, others, and ourselves. These judgments, when left unchecked or when based on false perceptions of the ego, entrap us in cycles subject to distortion. The issue isn't the parameter itself, but rather the way it's used, the way expectations are warped and not shifted into a healthier, more promising (and real) view. Instead of maintaining the parameter—learning to let go and view things clearly—we simply preserve the ego, attaching ourselves to what the ego fixates on.

This ego, with its judgments, influences how we perceive and conceptualize the world, manifesting as reactive and conditioned judgments that extend beyond the fundamentals. These verdicts, in most cases, must be right and display a sense of perceived superiority or inferiority, contributing to the ego's inauthentic and detrimental exaggerations of reality.

It dissects and categorizes things as good or bad, this or that, and these judgments shape our reactive conception of desirability. This ongoing process can trap us in a cycle of negative thinking that can last a lifetime. You judge people when you don't need to, you obsess over objects, knowing deep down that this is unwise, and you dwell in self-criticism, knowing it does nothing but hurt you.

The more you exist through the overly developed, exaggeration machine, the less you live through observant appreciation. In other words, the less you can live through unconditional connection with a consistent sense of happiness. It becomes more than just a mental process; it becomes your replacement. What you are is now overridden by this faculty, and a multitude of moments that could have been respected for what they are get run through this mental process and lost. The good news is that all the while, the real you is always there, watching and waiting.

That is not to say that every thought is a harmful form of judgment, or that every thought can be seen directly as a judgment alone. However, look closely and you will see that even ordinary thoughts originate from some sort of opinion, an unnoticed negative judgment, or a previous rash verdict. Most of the mind's content originates from there, beginning and continuing through analysis and stories.

The easiest way to spot the ego is in anything that creates a feeling of separateness, mentally and emotionally. This separation is precisely what the ego and its judgments do, from the smallest of thoughts to the total self. The feeling of fulfillment is the ultimate want; separation is the lowest means to this end. Whenever the ego can detach from your true existence, it will become more dependent on it, and the absolute awareness will be covered that much more. This can and will continue until the dissecting and dichotomizing mind gains complete control, fragmenting your existence into thousands of labels of wants, dislikes, and confusion.

The desire for this lost state of fulfillment manifests as the longing we feel. The ego, with its conditioning and narratives, repeatedly fails to satisfy this desire, as it attempts to achieve fulfillment through fleeting pleasures from external sources. Unaware that fulfillment is our inherent mode, the ego (the very source of separation) sees itself as separate from the cause of its dissatisfaction, perpetuating an endless series of seeking and attachment.

Over time, we evolve into beings of judgment defined by a collection of essentially meaningless pleasures and displeasures, rooted in dependency and desperation. This creates and sustains content that needs manipulation, leading many into tumultuous cycles of apathy, guilt, anxiety, and anger. This is characterized by poor actions, negative self-talk, and alternating phases of stress and relief. In efforts to cope, some individuals may even turn to substance addiction. As we age, it's common for men and women to become jaded and indifferent toward others. These states are not inherently good or bad, but they are often pushed to extremes, obscuring the path to a conscious and introspective life.

Quest for Authenticity

Imagination isn't creativity. Creativity is the higher ability to recognize and expand upon patterns— imagination may reflect this, but it can just as easily reflect any concept, memory, or unconscious compulsion. Creativity is not the act of conjuring thoughts at random, but the ability to refine, shape, and expand upon what already exists.

It's the one who holds the cold steel of reality who is truly creative. Those who understand that imagination is not unique, who see through the trap of needing to feel special or right, and who, through the investigation of their wrongness, learns to relate to others in deeper waters. Spontaneity plays its part, but this is only the recognition before inspiration takes hold. The creative mind doesn't waste itself in the fool's game of being original or unoriginal, it simply moves with what *is*, recognizing its pattern tendencies without grasping for validation. They know they stand on the shoulders of giants.

Authenticity lies not in the forced novelty but in presence—the ability to observe, to flow, to shape hyperreality into entertainment, knowledge, or simply connection. Whether for the masses, a friend, or a child, creativity bends the unreal into something meaningful. But hyperreality is never their mode of being; it's only a tool to be wielded, never a world to be lost in.

If you ever hear anyone or find yourself saying things that deviate from reality, and the belief is held strongly, that's one way the ego uses imagination, and it can be incredibly destructive. The ego must be right, which means even imaginary details will be seen as correct. Often, when this is questioned, the fear of uncertainty arises (fear of fear), and soon, anger and pride reveal themselves, refusing to change.

From the person who cut you off on the highway to your partner never paying attention to you, to the belief that *nothing ever goes your way*—these are delusional fantasies crafted by the ego. It's not an over-rationalization to spot the fallacy in these thoughts and emotions; it's self-awareness. Who knows why someone cut you off? But it's likely there was no vendetta against you. Is constant attention from your partner necessary or even desirable, and do you always give them full attention every second? As far as *nothing ever going your way,* chances are you're ignoring the little things that do go your way. Count your blessings, release the self-imposed suffering, and move forward with grace. Maybe life isn't as terrible as your ego believes.

To be more authentic to yourself is to be closer to reality and more in tune with your emotions, leading to better self-control. The worst part isn't the situations that arise, but the statements that perpetuate and reinforce the negative belief attached to them. When you reinforce nonsense aloud and within, you start losing trust and respect, and much more. Your ego gains power by creating distance from reality, and it's noticeable. Authenticity comes from not allowing that distance, from speaking and feeling only what is directly true in its various forms. Hear the senselessness in your words and be aware of what is in your control.

Understand how unrealistic expectations of others and favorable circumstances can be. Take a lesson from the Stoics: breathe in spirit and breathe out poise. Shift what you say in your head to only reflect what's authentic, or better yet, say nothing at all. Genuine authenticity comes from within and stays within—embrace the singular reality.

When questioning the mind, hunt down any dogma. Focus on every thought that has an unbendable quality, and question it until all nonsense is gone. You will soon see that the concretization of thought patterns has ensnared and sealed you under the ego. These types of thoughts, whether you're trying to be spiritual or simply healthier psychologically, should be shifted or eliminated. If you do this enough, you will realize that positivity is much more natural and realistic than negativity; negativity is just easier.

Dispute the thought and bring it back to reality; then practice: take a mental pause after recognizing the flow of the ego, scan it from its source, and expand into the quiet.

The goal of most psychological help techniques is to recognize inauthentic, dogmatic modes of thinking to prevent states of dwelling, a method pioneered by Albert Ellis in REBT (Rational Emotive Behavior Therapy) and others in similar styles. You can also find a relatable philosophy in the writings of the great and true hero Marcus Aurelius, as expressed in his famed *Meditations*. By addressing these thought patterns, you'll not only shape a healthier personality but also progress more smoothly through deeper spiritual practices, with fewer blockages in the way.

Examples of Inauthentic Thinking

Now that we've discussed how imagination and distorted thinking can pull us away from our authentic selves, let's explore a few examples of inauthentic thoughts and ways to think about and shift them into something more grounded in reality.

I hate myself.

How can you hate yourself? Are there two of you? This thought is not only destructive but fundamentally false. There is only one of you, and hating yourself creates unnecessary, dualistic conflict. Directly after you catch yourself saying something of this nature, you can say "no, I love my personality," as a quick rebuttal, or better yet, ask "who hates me?" Sense the regret, but don't let it define you; in Step Two, we will discuss how to better understand the emotion. As for a more logical replacement statement, perhaps "There was a mistake, and now it's time to move on and work to be better." Go forward with the intent of indifference to whatever situation happened, and know it is pure egotism to "hate yourself."

Nobody loves me.

Really? Nobody? Even if that feels true, or even is, it's not necessary for others to love you for you to find value in yourself. Endless love can be found within if you look hard enough and let the outside world rest. A more authentic thought might be, "I feel like I'm not being appreciated right now, but I know true love is not conceptual and comes from within." While this might sound like just an affirmation, remember that affirmations are more aligned with reality than self-pity. Over time, addressing and resolving these statements will yield genuine emotional progress.

I should have done that differently, I'm an idiot, and I can't do anything right.

Mistakes are a natural part of life, but self-blame doesn't help. Instead, try "I could have done that differently, and next time, I'll try to improve." There's no need for harsh self-criticism. Focus on effort, not perfection. This shift represents self-compassion, a more authentic and sustainable way to grow. Notice that most of the harshest sentiments we give ourselves revolve around some form of regret or guilt? Always choose self-acceptance over regret and shame—always, every time. A better replacement is "Things happen."

I have to get that thing done.

Reframe this as "I want to get that done." This simple shift eases unnecessary pressure. There is no situation where you *have to*, or *must*, do anything—it's about choosing to act with purpose rather than obligation. Be sure to use the word *'want'* instead of *'should,'* as it is both more motivating and realistic. Again, what you *should* do is complete opinion; you actually *want* to do it, whether you feel like it or not, is another question. This is also true with the term *can't*, such as "I can't do that thing," no, in reality, you *won't* do that thing." *Can't* is an arbitrary term disassociating responsibility from the amount of effort required to learn something or simply do the thing.

Everyone is a louse!

If you have nothing nice to say, say nothing at all (even mentally). Better wording might be, "I'm irritable today, but what others do doesn't need to be my priority." Remember, you alone are in charge of your emotions.

These are just a few examples of the habitual and problematic thoughts that might repeat. Watch for key words like *must, have to,* and *can't*—words that might carry rigid, dogmatic thinking. Be especially mindful of pairing these with blatantly negative words, such as *'hate,' 'stupid,'* or *'failure.'*

By catching and breaking these inauthentic thought patterns, you disrupt your ego's grip on your thinking and move toward greater self-awareness. Each time you reframe and/or dissolve an inauthentic thought, you weaken the ego's hold and take a step toward dissipating the judgments that keep you trapped in cycles of separation. This creates more space for authentic connection and ease in your spiritual practice and, in general life.

Remember, in our practice, we *are* still striving to break from the ego to a much higher extent. Simply watching for negative patterns of self-talk and inauthenticity, and actively working to address them, creates a habit of self-improvement in a more widespread sense and gets the ball rolling. However, still maintain an increased level of separation from your ego by denying this false self and creating mental gaps.

Hold closer to principles over ego. Principles, like respecting others and yourself, and prudence, over emotional and egoic servitude. Staying true to commitments like these helps guide you in the virtue of temperance. The ego in general is just talk. Too often, it is just trying to fortify its existence in self-absorbed pessimism. Keep from being one of the pitiful who say reality is sad. Sure, there is darkness in a compensatory life, and there can be elegance in that expression, but a general outlook is only miserable if despair is your mode of being. Desperation is only the quality of grasping at the world by something that has forgotten itself. Negativity is not knowing reality; it's a commitment to ego.

Opinions on Opinions...

To deny judgment as a part of nature would be wrong, but the person we seek to be makes judgments from a less conceptual place. In this place, we trust our virtue to shine as it will. Petty and personal judgments only reveal how deeply attached we are to our false perceptions. When you judge another person based on superficial concepts, it's a reflection of the ego, not truth. Though there is a reality of appearances and exuding strengths, these habitual judgments of endless condemnations do nothing to serve you, or the person being judged—it only strengthens the wall of separation between you and others.

The ego thrives in opinion because it maintains the illusion of separation—one person better, another worse—reinforcing the ego's need to feel superior. By observing this tendency and moving past engaging in unnecessary judgment, we weaken the ego's influence. In this, we meet all others as equals, and need not accidentally convince ourselves of being unwelcoming to others.

There are moments when someone may seek your help in times of turbulence; even then, it's worth considering whether you need to respond at all. You're on the path of the spiritual, and though others may misunderstand this and mistake it for what it is not, it is, above all, the thing to hold true to. Sometimes silence can be what's best for you. Don't be afraid to lend a helping hand, but recognize unnecessary drama and act through presence and clarity. When in doubt, act, but don't look down on prioritizing your practice of presence over anything else.

As you deepen your practice, you may find that many of the critiques you held onto were not as crucial. As you drift from ego, so does the view that another is ego. If you feel taken advantage of and need to address it, certainly do what you must. However, in general, try to recognize judgmental thoughts and focus on the practice, avoiding unnecessary verbalizations of criticisms. This approach is not about voicing every concern to relieve personal tension, but about mentally letting go first. Of course, there will be times when the pressure becomes too great and you may speak out, which is okay—you practice self-acceptance, after all.

Living as the ego means you see people as mere labels defined by that framework and your momentary feelings toward them. Instead of acknowledging their true essence—absolute peace—you perceive them as separate egos. When you exist too much as judgment, you must constantly be preparing for battle or feel the anxiety of the next conflict with any given person—a war can be waiting around every corner.

As you begin to let go, people who are still unconscious may not understand the changes you're making. They might even become upset that you're no longer engaging in the judgment games they're accustomed to, such as blaming, hypocrisy, or playing the victim, and they might think something is wrong with you. That's okay. Continue to be the light. Although they may not recognize it at first, they will, in time, be drawn to your radiance. Or they won't. However, the value lies in who you are, not in what people think.

In general, try not to take offense. You might feel as though you're standing up for yourself or speaking your mind, but all this is doing is giving someone else complete control over you. They're in charge of your emotional state, whether they want to be or not. Your emotions are now based on what someone else does, feels, thinks, and says. This is where a toxic relationship can begin and grow; giving another control when they don't want it will cause an undercurrent of resentment, especially if the emotions are consistently volatile.

Resentment at any level—from a mean boyfriend to the murderer of a boyfriend—gives another person control over you from within. It's in the desperation for control where you paradoxically lose the control—perhaps try reversing this paradox?

Ask yourself: What results from holding onto these mental positions, or from engaging in verbal attacks and defenses? How often do you end up regretting these actions, feeling remorseful for how you treated others or yourself? Or what seems accomplished? There are times for aggression, but mental aggression out of servitude to the ego solves nothing and creates too much unwanted emotions and despair, either buried or on the surface.

In these obsessive or volatile moments, your potential for using your mind for better purposes is usurped by the ego and its negative thoughts. You become imprisoned. Choose freedom instead. Rather than succumbing to a life ruled by judgments of desperation, strive to live through loving self-acceptance, extending to others through the view that there is only one (obscured) universal self. Only by freeing yourself from constant judgments can you truly find fulfillment.

Begin by recognizing when an episode of egoic dwelling ends, which may occur immediately after the first thought or several thoughts later, spanning from a minute to hours or even days. Strive to catch these moments more quickly each time. The important thing is to realize it happened, acknowledge it, and grow to understand it, knowing that this reaction is not a reflection of your true self. To reinforce this understanding, wait for the next habitual thought and observe your mind. Notice where the judgment originated. The one doing the observing—that is the real you. The space in which you wait is presence, and is what you aim to cultivate and embody more fully.

Self-Judgment

The most harmful form of judgment, which reverberates into all other negative emotions, is *self-judgment*. While it's natural to evaluate your actions and essential to take accountability and be honest, what we seek to transform are the repetitive thoughts that lead to guilt, shame, and resentment. Dwelling on these thoughts accomplishes nothing but clouding your intuition and, at times, even giving in to someone else's desire for you to suffer. It's in the dwelling of trying to solve the problem of you, but you, as ego (the problem creator itself), will fail this goal. We call this dwelling *regret*, and by disengaging with regret, we begin to stop using the mind's repetitive nature where it doesn't belong.

When you stop judging yourself, it may initially feel like a form of egotism, but it's not self-centered. I reiterate, that selfishness expects and has a need to feel superior to others, while self-love seeks inner peace. By committing to not judging others, not being offended by others' judgments, and, importantly, not judging yourself, you are choosing love over the ego. If you didn't take accountability or care about how you treated someone, driven by a sense of comparison, that would be different. But here, we are dropping judgment altogether because the mental dwelling it causes is hurting you, and perhaps even the people around you. It allows others to control you, and typically, these judgments stem from fabricated narratives rather than genuine reasoning.

In most personal situations, actual reasoning doesn't require deliberate thinking when judgments are needed; it's innate. Many mistakes would be avoided if we lived from a state of non-judgmental presence. If you worry that this mindset could lead to carelessness, rest assured that the opposite is true. Your reactions will transform into deliberate actions, and your judgments will become clearer and more focused, free from the influence of shifting emotions that could cloud decision-making.

To Hide, and The Tree of Life

In the famed creation tale, God's first molds, Adam and Eve, defied His warning and ate from the Tree of Knowledge of Good and Evil—committing what is known as the original sin. In that moment, their eyes were opened, and shame took hold; they hid themselves and covered their nakedness, unwittingly revealing to the Lord the forbidden knowledge they had taken. In response, they were banished, relinquished with the sacred curse of judgment as their own. With this curse, humanity was cast into a world of depravity, greed, cruelty, and war.

It's within this need to hide and cover that the seeds of inward judgment are found. You see it in our guilt, anxiety, deception, depression; within the tight imprisoning boundaries of the neurotic and the soul bound and ensnared by the weeds of self in the narcissist. Fear distorts thoughts, turning them into convincing, talking snakes. We may fight back in anger, and sometimes even win small battles, but the truth is the fear was induced by the self, and the fight sooner or later turns into an unwinnable war with oneself. And so, it goes—the easier, more enduring choice is to hide, lashing out when not allowed to cover yourself away. Like a wild Ape seeking the nearest tree of escape, but there's no hiding from this other, judgmental self.

But it wasn't Eden at the core of what was lost to judgment. There stood another tree in the garden— The Tree of Life, which God shielded from human touch with a flaming sword. This tree bears the fruit we, searchers of reality, strive to grasp. To obtain it, you must endure the tribulations of a societal existence and rectify the mistake of that forbidden knowledge, cooling and stilling the flaming sword. This resignation clears the path back to the essence of life, to Eden within, offering a chance to reclaim the Absolute that was lost.

Judgments don't just permeate in relationships, objects, or any ideal—they infiltrate everything you are, splintering you away from life's original warmth and calm. It starts as a measuring scale, then cracks and breaks into a hanging pendulum, swaying in the winds of emotion and vulnerable to a storm's fury. This is a life through the egoic judgment parameter— one that has yet to rediscover the truth. Be brave, and stubbornly grasp that Tree of Life within.

Past and Future

The ego finds comfort in misery and clings to wishes and nostalgia. The mind mistakenly dwells, while the heart endures great pain. Deep within, something in you rejects this suffering, and your thoughts revolt with endless questions and reactions. Yet, nothing is more potent than the present moment; there is no place more crucial than here and now.

You'll notice that most of your thoughts reside in the past or future, often leading to a harmful and significant waste of time. While time has its practical uses—such as scheduling or communicating—beyond its practicality, it also expands narratives, self-made problems, judgments, and everything else that constitutes the ego. Without memories and anticipations, the ego loses its places to dwell. By disengaging from the concept of time, suffering begins to dissipate.

So often we hope that uncovering our past will lead to a breakthrough, that understanding our conditioning will offer a cure. Yet, the real remedy lies in appreciating the present moment; then we can begin to let go of lingering problems and end cycles of dwelling. Recognizing what triggers harmful reactions is helpful, as it demonstrates a strong desire for growth, something inherently positive. After all, significant change requires deep aversion, but living in a solution-oriented way is essential.

Constantly creating stories and dwelling on memories projects a self that never resides in the one authentic reality, leading to an escalating sense of fear. Even our most accurate memories are colored by emotion and rarely reflect the truth entirely. Typically, these recollections don't influence the present productively; instead, they cloud the moment and hinder progress. As for future projections, they exist only in the imagination, anticipated through the lens of past experiences, present conditions, and momentum.

When you continually strive for more, craving extravagant results in another time, you live in a state of constant wanting. While you might obtain material objects that provide temporary satisfaction, it creates a habit where greed and desire dominate, and the allure of results overshadows the value of meaningful action. Without learning to find satisfaction in the present, you'll never experience a true sense of fulfillment, leading to confusion and eventually an identity crisis. However, embracing the present moment doesn't mean losing your purpose; instead, your purpose will become more authentic. Living from presence can unleash creativity and enhance the joy found in pursuing your goals. After all, doesn't a surge of creativity often feel as though time has stopped?

Whenever you find yourself projected into the past or future, take a moment to notice this shift. Recognize that dwelling on thoughts tied to time will inevitably create feelings of inadequacy and obscure your view of reality. Observe these thoughts, then pause and watch your mind, always aware that you exist beyond the confines of time.

Focused Action and Freedom

It should be noted, particularly in reference to the passage in the introduction about my personal relationship, which influenced my awakening, that although realizing the detriment of focusing excessively on another's emotional state was important, the key to overcoming this obstacle was *acceptance and letting go of outcomes.*

This principle mirrors the core teaching found in the *Bhagavad Gita*. In this famed Hindu scripture, while on the brink of battle, Krishna advises Arjuna (who is in doubt) to abandon attachment to results and complete what is his chosen duty. This relatable text, which can be read in just a few hours, reiterates a truth that has been echoed across various cultures and remains relevant today. In discovering this truth in my own way and adopting the practice of releasing mental attachment to past and future outcomes, I found a powerful tool for progress, and I advise the same for anyone.

To stay at peace while performing daily duties, without focusing on what will come of these duties—whether it be husbandry, work, or the time taken to chase a dream—is also called karma yoga. Karma is the basic, unavoidable cause and effect of the universe, perhaps related to what some today might call determinism. From the functions of the brain, the pendulum of thoughts and emotions, and the actions thereof—to a comet on the other side of the galaxy on course to the other side of the universe, and all the results—this is karma, fate. It's the hook, the fish, digestion, and the soil. It's the container and the contained, the freedom and the chaos, responsibility and law. Where there is pride, there is hurt; where a need to be right, there is a wrong. Where there is past and future, there is regret and anticipation. Accept what is as it is, leave the conceptual karma behind, and move beyond manipulation.

Just as Arjuna feared the murder of his kinfolk in battle, his duty was already in motion, and the war was inevitable. To run would only be an attempt to manipulate the unavoidable in hopes of augmenting his emotions; it would go against his chosen path and obligation. It's to hide where there's no place to hide. Krishna advised him to move forward. Focusing on what may result in good or bad, without accepting things as they are through reason, is to remain entangled in the cycle of karma. The more you practice being present, the more you will naturally move away from selfishness, so this should not be a concern. Be at peace with a quiet mind in the present moment and become spiritually formidable on a path of the enlightened.

To move beyond karma is to obtain freedom. Holiness is found in allowing good and bad to balance naturally, while evil lurks in attempts to manipulate this balance. In the realm of good and bad, what is considered holy and evil lie at their respective opposite ends: holiness embraces full acceptance and sacrifice, transcending the flow of balance into heaven, into freedom; while evil, deluded by self-indulgence, manipulates under the pretense of goodness (either to themselves or others), remaining fully entangled in conceptual karma. True freedom isn't only knowing that all is determined; it's handing mental karma, or conceptual time, over to the moment. In this way, you defeat the darkness of the conditioned mind.

Compulsive Submergence

Imagine a world where children are taught that to live a good life, they must continuously submerge themselves under water, moment after moment, holding their breath as long as possible. The longer they stay submerged, the more they believe they're growing. So, they dive deep, emerging only briefly for air and sunlight before diving back under again. As they grow, others add weights to their shoulders— sometimes out of necessity, sometimes because others don't want to bear the weight themselves. All this, demanding mastery of submergence.

Some become so skilled at holding their breath that they begin teaching others the art of submersion, believing they have found the key to life. They may even create new techniques, such as taking extra breaths before sinking back down. It is also possible that they become so skilled that they learn how to profit from being extra competent in non-breathwork. Here, breathing in itself as a means of fluid experience is often neglected and even ridiculed by many members of the diving public.

Imagine, too, a common belief that only after death will they no longer have to hold their breath, trusting a deity will keep them above the water after they die, allowing them to breathe freely forever. Additionally, others suggest that if you spend your life submerged in improper ways or don't come up for air enough, you are destined to live eternally being held under, without ever experiencing air and sunshine again.

What if, instead of waiting for death, we practiced living in the sunshine now? What if we breathe freely and embrace life as it is, above? The strong connection to life, growth, and communication is what makes us human, yet the compulsion to think without restraint has an unmistakable, drowning quality that requires an awakening to.

The endless submergence into compulsive thinking inevitably gives birth to external attachments. Grasping onto the insubstantial—whether materials or individuals—for a false sense of momentary fulfillment is just a byproduct of repetition with a separating ego. Whether positive or negative, whatever is continually given attention will take its place and become ingrained in our commitments. However, if we learn to curb this compulsion, we can break free from these attachments, introducing a path to a life of wholeness.

Compulsive thinking and attachments can lead to impulsive reactions, but with consistent discipline, impulsiveness can be weakened. Develop virtue and sharpen your attention to detail, using wisdom and presence to overcome the traps of conceptual time. This practice aims to transition from a reactionary, attachment-driven existence shaped by duality to a calm response-oriented approach that operates through a singular, absolute awareness. This transformational shift involves reclaiming the mind as a tool, rather than your identity.

These recurring thoughts shape how you interact with people and situations, especially if they're connected to those very thoughts. This can lead to unconscious negative interactions that feel justified or natural at that moment, only to be followed by regret and self-reproach, doubling the mental strain. This drain affects not only you but also those around you. Thinking depletes vital energy, and negative thinking even more so; the worst is the cycle of repeated negative thoughts. Repeated negative thinking becomes a pervasive, never-ending cycle of pessimism, overshadowing even happy moments with an inevitable return to negativity.

For many, the weight of constant negative thinking (dwelling) can make life unbearable, making death seem preferable to living trapped in a cycle of harmful mental patterns. This trap is born from a lifetime of compulsive thinking, now compounded by the habit of dwelling on unwanted thoughts. To break free, you must stop inventing problems, stop repeating negative cycles, and cease being a compulsive thinker and reactor. Let everything be as it is and appreciate every breath, living with a consistent sense of release. The true death needed is the death of the part of you stuck in draining conceptual repetition.

The habit of thought itself must be dropped, reclamation of the mind from its endless loops. Start by paying close attention to every thought, especially the negative ones. Embrace the stillness that comes after a thought passes. When you notice a thought repeating, challenge it immediately. Remind yourself: "I don't repeat thoughts; it's unnecessary and a waste of time." Then, redirect your focus inward and wait in the quietness of your mind.

The path to freedom begins by becoming a philosophical observer of your mind. Cultivate a mindset that is ready to let go of constant mental churn. My journey began when I realized that my happiness was too heavily dependent on others, leading me to recognize how external factors influenced my well-being. I began to distrust the conditioned responses of my mind, identifying and challenging every thought tied to negative emotions (which was beneficial for my practice, because most were). By embracing presence and waiting for the next thought, I sought to end mental dwelling. Initially, my goal was simply to escape the negativity I was trapped in, which I now recognize as a noble endeavor. Over time, I sought to silence all thoughts, recognizing patterns where even mundane or initially positive thoughts would spiral into negative dwelling (being in quite a sorry state). I wanted thoughts to exist only with my explicit permission. By quieting my thoughts, I grew closer to knowing who I was, and, as has been taught by many, I came to understand a deeper truth: "The root of suffering is a lack of self-knowledge."

Recap

Start by cultivating a deep awareness of your thoughts, especially the negative ones. Let these thoughts guide you as you explore their origins, turning them into a tool for deeper self-understanding rather than a source of distress. Notice how thoughts repeat without purpose, revealing you're the observer—awareness itself—rather than a mere victim of compulsive mental habits. Know the fantasies of time, and that this moment is the one reality. After you have pointed out a thought and inquired upon it, watch your mind from whence it came, see how it is not you but an object that too can be watched. Wait there lightly, with a questioning attitude, and anticipate the next thought with intentional attention. It will struggle to surface; simply wait for that next thought to arrive. In this awareness is who you are.

This step aligns closely with the practice of self-inquiry, a spiritual method famously advocated by the sage Ramana Maharshi. His approach, centered on the question "Who am I?", invites you to turn your awareness inward, seeking the truth beyond the mind's surface. Although I initially approached these practices independently, I later discovered how closely my journey mirrored the teachings of Ramana Maharshi, and further back to the Upanishads and everything in between. If you haven't yet explored this wisdom, I highly recommend it as a valuable complement to this practice.

Consistency is key. Make your practice enjoyable and aim to catch thoughts more quickly over time. Don't stress about when you catch a thought—focus instead on what you do, and the effort you put into the practice. Identify the strategies that work best for you and stick with them to help prolong the mental pauses.

Explore various types of thoughts and their connections to emotions. I've pointed out how I see the mind works to illustrate how negativity can proliferate and how to engage with your thoughts. There's much more to uncover—details specific to your personal patterns, desires, memories, and anticipations. Embrace the role of being your own philosopher and enhance step one with your insights, while ensuring they aren't self-serving.

It's important to distinguish between judgment and objective observation. While I advise against judgmental, repetitive, and time-bound thoughts, I encourage you to observe these thoughts objectively. This process of observation—rather than relying on personal judgment—allows you to distance yourself from the ego's compulsions, providing clarity and reducing fear. Remember that the shell of the personal self never gets completely discarded; it will be there, ready to be picked back up. This is why cultivating good virtue and quiet wisdom is important, not just because it is a practice, but also because it creates a more manageable and guided personality. This will benefit yourself and others greatly, simply having and holding the correct view will bring about positive change in character.

Before moving on to step two, take your time—dedicate at least a couple of weeks to mastering this technique. Consistency is crucial, and the more you practice recognizing and addressing your thoughts, the more natural the process will become. Aim to reduce the time between recognizing thoughts, ideally within an hour, and fully understand the process of observing and waiting until it becomes second nature. Remember, this is not a race, but a journey toward lasting inner peace.

"Where there is the tree of knowledge there is always paradise, so say the most ancient and the most modern serpents."

"Love is beyond good and evil."

—Friedrich Nietzsche,
Beyond Good and Evil

In this meditation, there will also be a focus on breathing, in conjunction with the paradoxical intention method.

Begin with a few simple, natural breaths. No need to control them—just observe the breath as it is already.

Now take two or three slightly slower breaths.
Let your shoulders relax.
Let your abdomen soften.
Allow yourself to sink into stillness. Let the breath carry you inward.

As you begin to settle, inhale again—but this time with focus. Feel the breath enter, and as you reach the top of the inhale, imagine a light energy drifting upward and away, like steam rising and drifting up from the momentum of the breath.
The energy floats, dissolves, and disappears...

As you slowly and comfortably exhale, gently shift your focus inward to your mind. With a light, curious attitude, begin the paradoxical practice: ask yourself,
"What will my next thought be?"
Watch and wait. Maintain a questioning attitude while allowing the thought to come, creating an observable gap in your thinking.

Feel free to breathe freely or take multiple breaths between the suggestions, so there isn't a sense of rushing. Come back to focusing on the breath when it feels natural in the progression of the meditation.

When a chosen exhale completes, place your awareness at the base of the belly. Feel any soft pulse of energy there—subtle, quiet.
Let your attention rest in that *stillness.*

Then softly return to the breath.
Inhale with the same spaciousness, feeling the movement of breathing, drifting with the energy.

Exhale into the paradox again, perhaps questioning right before the exhale: *"What will I think next?"*
Wait without force. Simply observe.

Repeat this cycle for several breaths—inhale into presence, exhale into the watcher.
Feel each breath quiet the mind and open the *space within*. Flow as energy.

When it feels natural, begin shifting your focus entirely to the breath, both inhaling and exhaling. Let the mind go quiet.
Rest in the rhythm of breath and the quiet energy at your core.

If thinking pulls too strongly and tries to reclaim center stage, return gently to the paradox: ask the question, wait for the answer, and notice where the thinker resides. *Is this you?*

Continue to allow attention to settle more and more into the breath and subtle energies of the heart and belly.
Let these be your resting place.

Close the meditation with a final, conscious breath—
calm, steady, and ordinary.
Then carry this state with you into life, as best you can, until you return to meditation.

— S T E P T W O —

BREATHE AND SURRENDER

To surrender is to give yourself up to the Absolute, moving beyond the ego. It's not to give up action or purpose—it's resignation of the emotional and mental resistance so cycles of suffering can end. It's to let go of negative emotions and the limiting conditions we've allowed to define us. If explained in highly spiritual terms, it's surrendering to one's inner spirit, to God. It's the decision to accept and flow with life, and let inspiration and creativity guide you. Surrender is spirituality, the highest practice.

The willingness to accept external problems and to navigate adversity and change rather than being stubborn and rigid is generally what we aim for in this step. In Step One, we addressed thoughts and introduced a simple yet highly effective meditative pause to help manage them. Now, in Step Two, we delve deeper into the core of spirit and well-being, learning to fully embrace the pauses and spaces in our thinking. By naturally releasing and transforming persistent negative emotions, we move beyond fleeting pleasures and enter a state of lasting peace and deeper fulfillment.

Most of our life is spent enslaved to the thoughts of the mind and the emotions that surround them. Aversion has become a powerful force because we've created an endless array of things to be averse to. It's time to mature beyond the attachments and irritations of a fearful, upset child and break through the self-imposed barriers that accompany these aversions. True fulfillment isn't found in satisfying desires or avoiding discomfort; it lies in embracing suffering and rediscovering a state of completeness that has long been buried.

The focus is on handling our emotions and engaging in conscious breathing. Remember to still use the techniques from Step One as a mental anchor to clear your mind when necessary. We're trying not to add narratives to emotional experiences, which can be challenging, especially if you find yourself in a relentless cycle of struggles, whether in relationships or other circumstances. However, the greater the suffering, the stronger the motivation. Let this suffering guide you; nothing highlights the need for change quite like genuine distress. Understand this and recognize that it can fortify you in previously unimaginable ways if you stay true to this practice. Over time, you might even find it exciting when a negative emotion surfaces, reminding you where you are and how far you've come in your progress.

Defeating Samskara

In my late twenties and into my thirties, I came to notice just how deeply samskara—the cycle of suffering born from clinging and aversion—had taken root in me. Every thought, failure, and disappointment had been repeating in my mind like a loop I couldn't shut off. I resisted emotions, tried to control outcomes, and pushed against the natural flow of experience. The more I resisted, the more suffering followed. This is the very nature of samskara: the ego's constant need to fix, grasp, and avoid.

At the time, I didn't have the language for it, but I felt the inner split: a mind driven by fear and desire clashing with something quieter, more truthful beneath it. That silent part of me wasn't asking me to control more, but to surrender that control. True freedom, I came to understand, isn't found in mastering the mind, but in letting go of its dominance. You don't escape samskara by winning its game. You step out of the game altogether.

Surrender is the only path that breaks the loop. Realizing I wasn't my thoughts wasn't enough—I had to release the need to follow them and believe in their urgency. When I did, peace didn't just arrive—it revealed itself as something that had always been there. Samskara begins to dissolve when we stop fighting what is and allow presence to take its place.

We Begin with Breathing

Beyond a tool for relaxation (or excitation), breathwork is a powerful practice to help focus the mind and enhance body awareness. The *conscious breath*, as it's known, serves as a source for retaining attention and giving the direct, physical sensation of *letting go*. Use each breath as a reminder to relax and allow the moment. This should be done right after you become aware of a thought, as part of the ongoing process of the first step. After you realize you are entangled in ego and recognize a thought, let the breath serve as a reminder to return to your practice, or simply use it to deepen and extend the practice.

Begin by inhaling deeply, preferably through your nose, slowly and steadily, while maintaining a comfortable position. Try to clear your mind during the inhales, focusing on the sensations of air entering your body after you've gained some presence, and enhancing your sense of the moment. Then, exhale at an easy, slower (or similar) pace, either through your nose or mouth, consciously relaxing your shoulders and abdomen. Let go of all mental efforts, allowing everything to be as it is. You can hold at the bottom or top of the breath cycle for a duration, or slow down completely with no struggle, feeling the inner energy in your belly and chest area, and expanding in this awareness. Repeat as many times as needed to maintain a clearer presence.

When in doubt, breathe. Let the breath guide you to presence. It can be observed that when you focus on the flow of your breath, on the rising and falling of the body, it becomes difficult to think at the same time. This is just one reason why it's such a valuable tool in the process of presence. Breathing, being at the forefront of your bodily functions and life, though usually automated outside the view of awareness, can be brought into awareness and purposefully shifted and focused upon, affecting your entire being right at its motor and through the nervous system.

To deepen your internal awareness, breathe into the space within you. Feel the expansiveness inside you and rest in the often-forgotten stillness. Awareness thrives in this stillness, and all energy flows through this internal space. Accept the space that exists as it is (understanding that space doesn't fluctuate with quantity) and become a patient observer from this quiet place. Feel what energy and space you can sense here. It doesn't matter if you feel anything special at that moment, just have a clear mind and a sense of allowance, with awareness of your inner body. If you do feel energy, feel it and continue in the same manner; nothing fundamentally changes, because no change is necessary. We're not in pursuit of great spiritual energy—we are the space that welcomes it, provided we maintain a calm mind free from overthinking, which otherwise obstructs it.

After some time of consistent growth in my own practice, while on my daily meditative walks at work to my car, I experienced something startling: while doing my normal breathwork, it suddenly felt like I wasn't breathing at all, as if my lungs and breath had become one with the air. As this occurs, it's surprising at first, you're confused if you're no longer breathing, but at some point, you realize you have slowed your breath down so much it feels, in an automated fashion, non-existent. It becomes untraceable to the human mind.

Outside these experiences, my breathing had slowed down significantly, approaching that same startling level. With control and consistency, this affects an integral function of your body, and in doing so, slows down (or speeds up) your overall functioning and the temperament of your mind, allowing it to become more malleable and focused.

Let your breath grow gradually slower through the total expanse of your practice. Integrate breathing with surrender. If feeling the rise and fall of your torso is too outside the idea of feeling your emotions, just imagine you are expanding and scanning the emotions you're accepting and letting go of, without considering the conscious breath as another step— only that things slow down while you do so, and this involves the breath.

Breathwork is a gateway to deeper focus and surrender. By linking breath with the practice of surrender, you create a powerful cycle of letting go, expanding your inner awareness, and welcoming a deeper connection to your true self. Each breath becomes a step toward clarity, toward letting go of resistance, and finding peace in the stillness of the moment.

Surrender

To surrender is to relinquish the ego and the repression of negative emotions, encompassing acceptance, letting go, and fully embracing the present moment within suffering, thereby yielding to your true self. Through this process, emotions also become clearer to observe, making it easier to check behaviors and adjust more comprehensively. Without the disturbances of overwhelming negativity and intrusive thoughts, we expand our sense of freedom and unlock our full spiritual potential.

Negative emotions are a habit formed through the mental connection of wants and circumstances. Similar to the style of paradoxical intention in step one, negative emotions grow in strength from resistance. They are, after all, a form of resistance in themselves. The reaction is then stored as a possible future reaction in similar circumstances, expanding with usage and deepening through the nervous effort to restrain it. There are, of course, unwanted strong emotions stored within memory, known or unknown at the mental surface, that bleed into certain things or all things you do. But this, too, can be augmented or even completely released through the habit of surrender, as long as detachment from the ego and its stories remains a priority.

It can feel as though you are releasing stores of negativity (and I'm sure it doesn't hurt to view it this way). This is because as we distance ourselves from the ego through surrender, we feel more fulfilled in authenticity, rising up the emotional latter through courage into wholeness. It's, in essence, the creation of a habit toward our true self. We are ending the perpetuation of reactive, negative resistance through acceptance and detachment from the stories associated with the emotion. We're actively short-circuiting the ego.

Mindfulness Scale

If I were to give a quick description of what that mentioned latter of emotional control would look like, it would be solely based on the distance from ego to the Absolute, and expressed in percentages (because why not?). Perhaps like this:

Zero to fifteen percent mindfulness:

Complete devotion to ego and mental conditioning, and in relating to all narratives one might tell themselves. The higher percent in these scales is just that much further from the ego. At the higher end on this level, there may be believers in mystical ideas and fortunetelling, particularly in the realm of personalities and their relationships. There is also a high priority in others in the form of gossip, and a strong sense of self-comparison. Most effort to be different from others is marked and marred by a surreptitious attempt to feel superior. The world be a significantly better place if only this level of consciousness were eliminated.

Fifteen to thirty percent:

Can be someone devoted to nature to an extent, or gaining interest in manifestation. Included are religious devotees who have an inkling of surrender. Someone might be in this realm and not be aware of mindfulness or spirituality, being drawn to nature, philosophical paradoxes, or creativity. Additionally, it can be those who are simply good at being happy or pursuing goals that align with their deeper selves. Spiritual awakenings may also be experienced here.

Thirty to fifty percent:

This can be considered the manifestation sweet spot, where you're still in tune with the person but open to suggestibility for a functional shift in attitude. Sometimes, housing a higher level of religious types, spiritual experiences can occasionally lead to fanatical ideals of the experience, strengthening the belief in their chosen religion. However, this isn't inherently negative, and surrender through a religious outlook can possibly take you to the highest level of this scale.

Fifty to seventy percent:

Where complete dedication to the self as within takes place. If someone is on this level, they have chosen a path beyond others and are fully dedicated to spiritual practice. Here, ideas of manifesting or deities hold no sway; there is only one Absolute presence understood. Practicing surrender and being present begins to become second nature, where the practice becomes just as easy as not practicing, or even easier. Emotions entangled in anger and apathy become near shadows of their former selves, and are hard to come by. Thoughts are almost all seen as one substance, being let go with no need for explanation.

Seventy to ninety percent:

Near complete effortlessness of practice. Inner words are only whispers, no negative emotion holds power, and bliss is a consistent standard of being. Peace over energetic rapture is preferred, and the possible distance of ego from spirit, or the real self, will be an everlasting dichotic view never to be dropped.

Ninety percent and higher:

Full realization, enlightenment. Plato's sun outside the cave. Pure consciousness as self, bliss. Effortlessness and the end of spiritual practice.

The stages of mindfulness I present are in no way perfect or clean-cut. Any number of occurrences can overlap, and every individual is working with their own conditioning and surroundings, including their layers of chemical makeup, so we all have a multitude of nuances to deal with. I am not saying anyone's belief in any religion or scientific sense of morality is unjustified; they are just specific shades of what makes up a part of the thing that has become a personality, and may or may not present difficulties or ease. We're seeking a self that transcends personhood and is universal; in whatever way this singular ideal is promoted with health and respect, it's a correct path.

The Practice of Surrender

When practicing surrender, breathe slowly and welcome the inner senses. Acknowledge any dark emotions that surface, sitting with them fully without layering on additional narratives of pain. Remember to use the technique from step one to distance your mind. It can help to become knowledgeable and skilled at identifying specific emotions—such as insecurity, guilt, grief, or anger—so you can better understand how they specifically feel, how often they arise, how intensely you experience them, and why they occur (we'll talk more on emotions specifically in the next section). Still, the key is to avoid letting any related thoughts or mental stories take control. Your emotions are the primary place of focus in the gaps, and it turns out they can hold focus very well. By knowing yourself in this way, you will be able to identify what to watch out for and handle it more rapidly and skillfully.

Focus your attention on the physical sensation of the emotion, often felt in the stomach or chest.

Notice the way it manifests in your body. Whenever your mind starts drifting back into mental narratives, gently return your focus to your breath—inhale slowly and exhale to release any doubt and the weight of the world. If you need help regaining focus, remind yourself that you are not your emotions. That emotion is simply passing through you. Return to a state of focus and calm awareness, and even become aware of that awareness to facilitate expansion. Start with each conscious breath, and remember that every breath can be a conscious one if you are determined to make it so. And, if you don't need a breath, don't take it, it's up to you.

Negative thoughts generate a harmful energy that perpetuates a cycle of avoidance and obsessive thinking. This mental battle and habitual negativity will drain your energy, leaving little for aspirations and positive relationships. Interestingly, the energies of apprehension and apathy feel strikingly similar to inner joy and elated peace, if you pay close attention to the sensations, despite their stark differences in attitude and direction. With time, presence, and surrender, negative emotions will transmute into lasting states of peace and joy.

In a way, instead of thinking of these emotions as opposites flowing on a spectrum, I think of these positive (peace, joy) states as relating to the natural state of consciousness, and the negative ones (apprehension, apathy, anger, etc.) as relating to the same source of energy but bent by the ego's mental sense of time and yearning—into painful emotions—a singular base presence (consciousness), distorted by different forms of mental resistance. So, defeat the ego—control the emotions.

First, become comfortable with this energy through self-acceptance. Then practice disassociating from your thoughts while in this state, which helps prevent rumination and allows you to exit the negative state with more lasting potency. Remember, this practice is not about repressing emotions—we permit them, not bury them. You lessen the strength of emotions by accepting and flowing with the feelings, so as not to be paradoxically increased by resistance. You end negative repetition by ending the emotion's direct attachment to thoughts, by disassociating them from their stories and expectations.

While it may seem difficult at first, and even more painful, emotional pain will soften and arise less frequently with this practice. If diligent, the most significant effects are noticeable as you grow spiritually deeper over time—be sure to reflect on your progress periodically, to give a boost of encouragement when needed.

Emotions really *do* begin to release their hold when they're felt in full presence. It's a freeing process, and contrary to what you might fear or expect, it doesn't cause any damage. It's known you handle what you fear by facing it, but for some reason, when it comes to emotions, there's an opinion that emotions deserve the fear that perpetuates it into self-absorption. But emotions do shift and dissipate, and they are not you; so, don't resist the fear, face it, and conquer yourself.

Mastering any skill involves repeated failures, and perfection should never be expected. Acknowledge the setback and continue moving forward. This resilience paves the way for an added transformative practice: releasing self-judgment. Let your response to setbacks become part of your practice—accept them and let them go, and soon you will find a more manageable overall state.

It can help to look back at a bad reaction and analyze what exactly happened. Did certain emotions spark certain thoughts, or vice versa? Objectively retrace the steps, from the rising emotion to the thoughts and actions directly preceding and following, and consider whether this is a habitual tendency. Do this with no intention of laying blame on any external factors. Is there any inauthenticity or dogmatic beliefs? Were there any irrational words used like "can't," "must," or "never?" What exactly is the emotion, and where is it in my body, and does it come about too often and too easily? Grow acquainted with the workings of your mind—understand what stirs your displeasures (and pleasures), and how the pathways of emotions and thoughts flow when unchecked. These considerations can be helpful, but as your understanding progresses, they should eventually fade away as your knowledge stands on its own.

In times of relationship difficulties or general life challenges, when the urge to express your thoughts feels overwhelming, take a moment to breathe and let the urge pass, creating space for it to exist without immediate reaction. Surrender to the moment. However, if keeping quiet feels like suppression, speak out, but consider the value of maintaining a calm and collected mindset, ensuring your response is balanced and thoughtful.

Whenever you speak a problem into existence by complaining or gossiping, you may unintentionally anchor yourself deeper into negativity, inviting, or worse, forcing, others into your struggles. While discussing problems can offer temporary relief, like massaging a broken leg, it rarely cures the root cause, and if anything, exacerbates it. In sharing your burdens in this way, you may inadvertently spread negativity, as misery indeed loves company. Rather than reinforcing these illusions, our goal is to dissolve them. We're here to transcend the ego, not to indulge it.

Surrender Often and Consistently

There will be plenty of opportunities along your path to practice surrender—embrace them all, even the simplest opportunities. Remember, this practice is not an instant remedy; it requires consistent effort that gradually leads to effortlessness and certainty. The ultimate goal is consistency—integrating this practice into your daily life and seizing every opportunity. Whether it's irritation from traffic, an argument, workplace stress, or a disruptive noise, use these moments to refine your skills. Always choose to release rather than react. The moment you remember to do so is the perfect moment to practice.

In my own experience, I began practicing surrender during periods of intense emotional turmoil. I aimed to maintain presence for as long as possible, allowing myself to fully experience and expand deeper and deeper into the emotion. Despite frequent initial setbacks, I persisted. Each time, I would restart with a conscious breath, seeking silence and space within my mind, and focus my attention on the internal fire that was too often ignited in my chest. I made this my practice whenever possible, increasing my effort by using the technique even during easier times, subtly digging for emotions, and bringing my attention to whatever surfaced.

Inner Light, and an Image of Love

Before long, I became aware of an inner light—a radiating, peaceful energy. I applied the same principles I used in times of distress, but instead to become more deeply aware of consciousness itself. I then combined this awareness with gratitude, further strengthening my practice. Through continuous surrender, I witnessed a profound transformation in my life. I was not just practicing; I was living a dedicated journey of change.

A technique I adopted during the beginning and middle of my practice was to have a general and repeating replacement image for a while, which might work for you. When I sensed a dark thought coming on, I would think of my daughter smiling and let that image be all there was, floating in and fading away. I tried to let whatever emotions were tied to the image flood my person. This thought helped craft and sustain my inner light. This also helped clear my mind in a motivating way, allowing me to softly dissipate a negative emotion. I chose this image because it was genuine and brought me the most joy, and I'm not interested in things of magnificent manifestation, although it can still be seen as a manifestation technique.

In this style, love is given the central meaning to life, both the thing to look forward to and to be embraced as the moment's inspiration. It provided a sense of purpose at that time that was perhaps needed, an understanding of the correct outlook that I would hope to consistently model in every experience. It's *strange*, if all life is the overcoming of the original dependence given by the parent, that so often that overcoming is, in a way, gifted by returning that dependence to a child. Undoubtedly, the great mediator, *responsibility,* plays its role alongside *love*.

However, if you choose to adopt this technique with the goal of manifesting something material, I recommend selecting an image tied to plausible actions toward achieving your goal, rather than focusing solely on the outcome. Focusing on outcomes can lead to fixation on results, which might not only hinder the manifestation process but also increase dissatisfaction from living a results-driven life. For instance, when I have recently used this technique, instead of dwelling on a fancy house or car, I imagine myself typing intently at my computer. This isn't about monetary gains but about feeling inspired while engaged in the act. As the image passes, what remains should be a sense of inspiration and fulfillment— meaning.

Here is an important tip to remember: *know the impermanence of negative emotions.* Emotions, like any other mental construct, are subject to the ebb and flow of opposites and dissipate due to their inherent lack of substance. Recognize that they come, and they go, and they don't have the power to destroy you on their own. The only real danger lies in the actions you take under their influence and the habits that form, leading to misconceptions about their permanence.

Keep this perspective in mind as you practice surrender. It can be especially reassuring when it feels like emotions are concealed or deeply rooted in your body. Remind yourself that there is nothing to fear; an emotion might be painful, but the discomfort is temporary and ultimately harmless.

Absolute Bliss and Fear

At the foundation of all emotional experience lie two basic emotions: *bliss* and *fear*. Bliss is the absolute and fulfilled state of consciousness—energy aware of itself, feeling complete unity and wholeness. Fear, on the other hand, is the desire for absolute bliss to continue without interruption or end. Fear is the keeper of bliss, necessitating survival, reproduction, and the pursuit of security to ensure that energy remains aware of itself (conscious) in a finite system.

Bliss

Inner joy, the feeling of unity, completeness, and harmony with oneself and beyond. Absolute consciousness. Relating to *peace, empathy,* and *inspiration.* It's the origin point of all positive emotional experiences. When someone entirely discards the ego, awareness of bliss is possible, and knowledge of life's source is apparent.

Fear

The awareness that bliss, or the ensuing minute

glimpses of bliss, will be lost or is limited by external conditions, and thus motivates the drive for survival and continuity. It can be seen as desire in its most basic form—the desire to maintain or extend bliss through life. It's resistance and attachment that prevent us from staying away from uncertainty and discomfort. Aversion is its clearest representative.

Desire

Fear manifests as a pursuit—grasping at things we believe will recreate or sustain fulfillment, or elements of it. It's the search for the Absolute. In its highest form, it's inspiration, and at its lowest, the sensual desires.

Attachment

Arises when a desire has been satisfied, and we habituate this satisfaction. The mind begins to identify certain objects, people, or outcomes as being necessary to maintain a taste of bliss, but they are still merely echoes of the original state. It can also be the sustaining of comfort, whether positive or negative, as a remnant of a past pleasurable experience.

From these fundamental modes of feeling, all other emotional states emerge. As fear, desire, aversion, and attachment intermingle through the ego in various ways, the other emotions emerge. These are not inherently negative, but rather represent the natural consequences of finite creatures with the potential for awareness of consciousness.

Happiness

The temporary result of a desire or attachment being gratified, its intensity varying based on how closely it mirrors true bliss. Sensual pleasure is the lowest form of this happiness—short-lived and rooted in sensory gratification—whereas peace exists on the higher end, closer to the original state of the Absolute.

Sadness

Arises when desires are thwarted or attachments are lost. This can be seen as manifesting in the sense that bliss in whatever degree has been lost or unattainable. Sadness often emerges as *regret* (a clinging to a lost past or personal mistake) or sustained *apathy* (a disconnection from the pursuit of joy).

Bliss, or the maintained current of inward joy, is the

source of all emotions. Fear, as the desire to sustain bliss, becomes the guardian of this state, of life. However, when fear becomes entangled with more rational thought, as it has with us, negative exaggerations emerge. The ego is essentially a distortion of fear and bliss, leading to misunderstandings that result in grasping at external things to recreate an internal state. This confusion leads to emotional blockages that hinder spirituality and prevent a return to absolute bliss. Although, without it, the full return possible for us (above all other animals) would not be possible in the first place.

A notable oversight in materialist philosophy, and one often found in modern science, is the failure to acknowledge the existence of absolute bliss. Science is a powerful tool for understanding the physical world, but its methods cannot account for the personal experience of bliss, of inspiration, and empathy in their purest, non-conceptual form. Philosophies that emerge solely from scientific reasoning are built by those who, more often than not, lack an inspired drive toward realization. Morals and social objectives become based on a composite style of conceptual compassion, and the inspiration (spirit) of the individual gets lost in the dispersal. As a result, consciousness as bliss—the unifying principle of all experience—goes unrecognized, relegated to a religious or dualistic context alone.

While science excels in explaining material processes, it remains bound by the subjectivity of the observer. Real consciousness, by its very nature, requires direct experience to be understood, and therefore won't be understood by someone closed off by egoic philosophies. It's not something that can be measured, categorized, or quantified within the parameters of a scientific test (at least not yet). As long as the unifying quality of bliss is ignored, the division between materialist and spiritual worldviews will persist.

Worse still, scientific reasoning, in its quest for facts, often disregards or seeks to dismantle what it cannot quantify: connection itself. Absolute bliss, the ultimate source of connection, defies material explanation. The drive for purely objective facts without a corresponding acknowledgment of what spirituality has to offer deepens the division between human beings and the universal consciousness. Faith in consciousness as the root self gets forgotten, and the ego becomes more accepted.

By surrendering the ego's desire for control, we reconnect with our deeper, inner source. This surrender is an active recognition of the inner truth: absolute bliss is waiting within, and fear's attempt to protect it through desire and attachment is unnecessary. By letting go, we uncover a realization that what we seek is already present, there to be fully experienced by anyone with the courage to do so.

Blockages to the Absolute

When we discuss surrender, we talk about letting go of resistance, mental burdens, and emotional attachments. But it helps to explore the specific emotional traps, or temperaments, that act as barriers to our progress—emotional modes we often cling to because they feel natural or even justified. Each of these emotions represents a corner of the ego's influence, but within each, there is an opportunity for growth through awareness and surrender. Understanding how to focus on and release these emotions is vital to moving beyond the ego.

Anger

Anger is like a poison or drug that, when taken, feels intoxicating because of the energy it can provide. It grows in habit fast, working on dopamine and feeding the obsession to be right, even falsifying the egoic sense of happiness at times. It can begin to hold unconscious value because of the results it seems to bring, especially in moments of manipulation or conflict. If you haven't noticed, anger is popular amongst children—it can push boundaries and get you what you want. However, nearly all values held at the level of ego are detrimental to our practice. Anger is a combination of fear and resistance, and if untamed, can bring with it a life of outward and inward abuse, making consistent disaster unavoidable, often in correlation with courage's fallacious cousin: pride.

Be aware of anger's fleeting nature. When we recognize that the energy anger provides is a false sense of control, we can choose to surrender the need to be right, allowing humility and acceptance to replace the toxic need to manipulate outcomes. This opens space for true strength through spirit—strength that doesn't need the artificial boost anger provides but thrives in clarity and inner peace.

Pride

Pride is a form of overcompensation for a lack of courage, in the interpersonal, self-fulfilling sense of pride. It hits down to prop itself up. Pride takes offense out of fear that its fear will be witnessed—a form of hiding. Pride seeks to mask vulnerability. Can a courageous person have pride? Most of us have some sense of pride varying in degrees, but the truly courageous person often has a lower level of pride, balancing it with humility and awareness.

If pride is the shield of fear, then the key is to face the fear directly. Rather than hiding behind offense and judgment, there is power in admitting weakness and accepting imperfection. Real courage requires stepping out of pride's false security and into authenticity. By treating pride as a defense mechanism, we move toward a deeper sense of self that doesn't rely on external validation. Step away from the ego inflation and embrace quiet inner confidence. This real courage will lead to more genuine connections with us and others.

Modesty

Modesty itself can also be seen as a form of masking fear—fear of being too much or too little. Too much modesty can become an overcompensation, a tool for rejecting desires or social misconduct under the guise of morality, which too often is met by missed opportunities, regret, and self-hatred. It's within the flux of accountability, specifically, the spectrum from the shameful to the shameless. The primary use of modesty, in our context, is to avoid scary situations for a self-conscious individual, in hopes of preventing judgments from others and a personal fall into guilt. Where high levels of pride with low levels of modesty (easily offended without a sense of accountability) may be the path of the narcissist, vice versa (self-effacing and ashamed) might be seen as the way to the neurotic. However, you can see the similarities in their self-absorptive characters.

The key to transcending the trap of modesty is balance: embracing modesty without letting it become a hiding place for fear or guilt. The modest person who knows their worth can navigate between humility and self-respect, grounded in an awareness that true worth is not dependent on inflated pride or excessive self-effacement. In finding this natural balance, true modesty becomes an expression of confidence, not a cover for insecurity. If you let go of regret, soon after it occurs, you find balance here.

It's good to remember that all existence is subject to compensation; this is the point of every chemical released in your body, in lieu of every judgment on every experience. Traits like pride and shame rest on spectrums that are what they are due to distortions of the ego, exaggerating what should be natural and adaptive. Without the ego's interference, no mediation would be necessary. In the absence of ego, balance is no longer something to manage—it's simply the natural state of being. You can view it as decreasing the spectrum of emotions themselves by reducing the element that causes the wide spectrum, the ego, creating natural balance and a more manageable state of being.

The remedy for character extremes lies in releasing mental attachment. By dropping the clinging that binds us to false identities—whether inflated or diminished—we gain clarity. Presence is the mechanism for this release. In stillness, the ego's sway fades, and the self corrects into balance. Modesty and pride, like all aspects of character, are harmonized not through effort alone, but through the grace of awareness.

Regret

Regret (including guilt and shame) is the mother of dark emotions. It creates a perfect example of the distortion dualism creates, as it often represents an emotion that is a mirage of another emotion—a distortion of unwanted reality. Regret has its obvious utility, as we need some regulation and accountability. Still, it becomes the ultimate ego failure when left unchecked, leading to an inability to regulate the entire system. When these bending emotions are allowed to dominate, depression usually follows. Unregulated self-judgment is at the heart of many mental and emotional struggles, fueling feelings of worthlessness and separation.

Regret must be met with radical self-compassion. Awareness of regret as an egoic construct—that arises from identifying too closely with our mistakes and shortcomings, through a need for perfection or rightness—allows us to shift our perspective. Instead of being consumed by regret, shame, and guilt, we can acknowledge our imperfection and move on. Transcendence here involves self-forgiveness. This isn't a superficial pardon but a deeper understanding that guilt, when objectified and released into the moment, serves as a guidepost for personal growth. We can integrate lessons from our past without allowing it to define us, and free ourselves from the endless cycle of self-recrimination. Regret is based primarily on conceptions; by tackling each defacing conception as it arises, we transcend further and further from the habit.

Apprehension

Apprehension, or anxiety, is regret turned forward—a worry about a future mistake, or a worry about future concern. Apprehension revolves around the anticipation of failure and the inability to trust the present moment. While guilt looks backward, apprehension looks ahead, locking the mind in a cycle of fear and hypervigilance.

It's a sign of attachment to a future we cannot control, or fear of ignorance. The cure to excessive anticipation is, almost obviously, presence (and knowledge to its necessary extent). When we become aware of the mental projection's anticipation creates, and its poor effect, we can anchor ourselves in this moment. By consistently practicing presence, we break the cycle of apprehension and its self-fulfilling loops. Accepting each moment as it is is the purest act of courage, allowing us to meet whatever comes with grace, rather than mental overwhelm. When regret and anxiety are left unchecked and mentally resisted, they spiral together into a state of depletion: relentless apathy, depression. Also, don't forget to breathe.

Depression, in the consistent overwhelming sense, is the result of accumulated emotional blockages like anger, pride, anxiety, and excessive guilt, within full identification with the mind. It's the weight of unresolved emotions, fueled by a strong habit of resistance, manifesting as consistent numbness or despair. But even depression, as heavy as it feels, is not immune to the power of surrender. Presence, breathing, and acceptance are the tools that can slowly dissolve the emotional layers leading to depression, freeing you from the cycle, one release at a time.

By staying conscious of each emotion as it arises and surrendering to the moment, you prevent it from building up into something more substantial and more complex to release. The aim, again, is not suppression but dissolution, allowing you to move forward with a lighter, fuller, and more centered self.

All these emotional modes represent an opportunity for transcendence through awareness and surrender. The common thread is the realization that these emotions are rooted in ego-constructs that can be observed, understood, and ultimately transcended.

By shifting from identification with these emotions to awareness of them, we enter a higher state of consciousness, one not dictated by fear, guilt, or pride, but rather by self-acceptance, courage, and presence.

An Experiment: Pillow Talk

Now, on a lighter note. Try this experiment, with a partner, alone, or just in your imagination (recommended). Grab a pillow and hold it out in front of you, with elbows locked straight. See everything around you but avoid focusing on the pillow, treating it as if it were merely an appropriate extension of yourself, to be ignored.

Hold this position for about ten seconds. Now, imagine your partner (or yourself) saying something offensive. Begin flailing the pillow at your imaginary partner, or at a nearby mirror. Continue the outburst for as long as feels natural. After you've finished, take a breather and lower the pillow to your hips, giving your arms a break. Soon after, raise your arms again, relock your elbows, and resume your original posture with the pillow extended.

As you hold the pillow out again, have your partner (or yourself) try to comfort you. Listen to their sweet words as they attempt to console you, the pillow remaining between you. Notice how much easier it is if they hug you from behind, for both convenience and safety purposes. If you want to add an extra element to the experiment, give your partner a pillow and have them flail about with you. Then, try to comfort each other while both of you hold your pillows out.

This pillow represents your habitual, suppressed, and repressed emotions that have been held within, lived with, but not fully accepted and let go of. The flailing was the pent-up energy boiling over, and the agitation was caused by resisting the negativity for too long. Over time, different thoughts become associated with these stored emotional responses, increasing the likelihood of a triggered episode and creating a vicious cycle of negativity that drains your energy.

Now, try a different approach. Hold the pillow out again, but this time consciously notice it along with your surroundings. Gradually focus more on the pillow until it captures your full attention. Breathe deeply, allowing the pillow to lower as your arms relax slowly. Let yourself take in your surroundings without the pillow blocking your view. Open yourself up to life, unencumbered by the strain of resistance.

If you're provoked again, stiffen your arms out, but instead of flailing, refocus on the pillow. Maintain your focus and breathe. Slowly lower the pillow again, eventually placing it on the bed where it belongs. See how much freer and more embraceable you become with arms wide open.

Surrender isn't about denying your emotions; it's about embracing them and allowing them to rest. Believing that all feelings are unchangeable is an incorrect view. See them at their roots—uncertainty, attachment, and resistance, and all the combinations that make them up. Uncertainty (fear) shifts when nothing needs to be certain; attachment loses its grip when you let it breathe; and resistance is relinquished through self-acceptance. Altering any of these—whether it's letting go of certainty, attachment, or resistance—will have a noticeable impact on the consistency, strength, and type of emotions you experience.

The Sacrifice

But beyond the simple release of emotions, there lies a deeper, more physical level of surrender—a barrier that no one on the righteous path can avoid. Surrender in its most valid form always asks for something more: sacrifice. This theme of sacrifice runs like a thread through the spiritual traditions of the world, carrying with it the weight of loss and transformation. One of the most potent examples comes from the story of Abraham in the Old Testament, where, like it has for me and so many others at some point, sacrifice took center stage.

In Abraham's journey, as he spread the word of God, he first had to conceal the truth about his beautiful wife, Sarah, pretending she was not his wife (but his sister), in fear that kings would surely kill him to claim her—a sacrifice in its own right. But, the real and dark test comes later—God asks him to sacrifice His gift to Abraham and Sarah, their son Isaac. Imagine the heartbreak, the internal torment, the sleepless night before, and the wrenching fear and angst of this divinely demanded choice. The struggle between love, faith, and obedience would surely tear anyone apart, as it did Abraham, who snapped into insanity at the moment of sacrifice.

Kierkegaard captures this internal battle beautifully in *Fear and Trembling*, where he famously reimagines 'The Binding of Isaac.' In this sermon, he later also describes the person who reaches the highest point in spiritual life as the "knight of infinite resignation." Abraham metaphorically (I think) reaches this point—willing to give up his son, his most cherished bond, out of faith. In the end, it is Abraham's willingness alone that proves enough. His son is spared, and a ram takes Isaac's place on the altar.

On my spiritual path, I've faced a relatable demand for sacrifice—less dramatic than Abraham's, of course, but emotionally turbulent in its own way. That story has since held a special place in my heart because I've felt its echoes in my own life. I've discussed how I learned to let go of other people's emotions, to stop clinging to outcomes I couldn't control. But my greatest challenge wasn't just letting go of the emotions of others—it was letting go of something even closer to my heart: the need to be present in my child's life, or put simpler, to lose my child (too often, for too many, the case is very similar).

For so long, the fear consumed me. It kept me tangled in emotional turmoil, making it impossible to find peace in that state. But eventually, I reached a point where I had to let go, completely. I had to allow that fear to play out if it had to, let go of the relationship with the mother and what would ensue, and stop fighting it. This was my Abraham moment, so to speak—my own version.

Allowing this darkness its space, no matter

how difficult, gave me the freedom and clarity to move forward in spiritual understanding. In surrendering this deep fear, this extraordinary resistance, I was no longer burdened by the emotional weight that had clouded my judgment for so long. As I grew stronger in spirit through this, I also eventually gained the space to make choices without being weighed down by external judgments or self-judgment; choices that were intuitively connected to the results I would have wished for in my previous state, but would have been too bind to recognize. It became clear that sometimes, to progress, we must be willing to let go of the things we love the most.

It's not just about surrendering to what is mysterious and powerful—it's about sacrificing all the external factors that are deeply entrenched in the mind, even the ones we hold most dear. For some, it might mean loosening the grip on a loved one or family member. For others, it could be the desire for external objects, such as wealth, sex, or status. And for those whose intellect has given them so much, the forfeiting of that intellect. To know spirit, you must become spirit, and to become spirit, all that is not spirit must be thrown away. To be what you were, to be that person, is no longer viable if the search for a soul, for God, is in earnest.

To achieve absolute consciousness, great sacrifices will be made. The deeper the desire to reach the Absolute, the greater the sacrifice required, leading ultimately to what Kierkegaard described as *infinite resignation*: the willingness to surrender everything, again and again, without end.

Recap

Always remember to incorporate a deep, conscious breath when needed. Inhale slowly through your nose if possible, focusing on expanding your abdomen, and exhale, allowing your shoulders to relax. This practice is amazing for maintaining presence or extending it. It's effective in assisting in any area of practice, such as when you need to drop a topic, let go of time, judgment, duality, etc. Try to engage with your inner energy during breathing, especially at the bottom and top points of the breathing cycle. If it feels like you're straining to focus too much on breathing, simply observe and use it more in the sense of flowing in and out of your inner energy and emotions, allowing it to fall back to an unconscious facilitator. If you find the breath unnecessary, don't worry—it's simply a tool to facilitate ease. However, if it consistently enhances your practice, as it did for me, make it a staple.

When in a high emotional state, acknowledge the emotion and do your best to avoid adding the story attached to it, using the method from step one and breathing. Surrender. Don't try to end the emotion through positive emotions. Take your time and feel what you are feeling, allowing it to exist as it has become over time through mental use. Let the process be objective, nothing else. If you think you have failed in any way, know that this is not true. The fact that you were aware of the mistake is a significant step. Let that sense of failure be another chance for the practice and to examine your mental habits. Always watch for that sense of regret, shame, or guilt and dissipate it, encouraging dwelling to end. Practice on all irritable situations—from the lowest degree to the highest— and also practice on situations that arise seemingly without thought, but from an unconscious negative dwelling. This is a good opportunity to get ahead of the emotion that causes negative thought patterns. Remember, no emotion is permanent.

During quieter moments, try to feel a light, joyful sensation around your heart area (at the center of where the breath rest), using a similar approach to handling negative emotions. Don't force it—just allow for space and let an unchanging stillness guide you. This practice gains potency with a clear mind. Allow this light to carry into all you do, and remember that at the bottom of all those negative emotions, this light can be found. It can be helpful to use a positive image to fade with the thoughts, reminding you in that moment of positivity and what you strive for; mine was an image of my daughter smiling up at me.

No intense emotion is permanent, nor is it an integral part of you. If a negative emotion, or a knack for aggressive reactivity, has become a staple of your personality, there's a good chance you're not getting the pity you think you deserve. This is because we all know, on some intuitive level, that personhood is nothing more than a carry-on in the ride that is life. If standing alone as consciousness, and with self-knowledge, is desired, that personhood must be dropped. To give up ego completely requires sacrificing all its attachments, from the small distractions to what we hold dearest. There is pain in this. And that pain is what must be unrestricted and accepted to become the Absolute, and you do this through surrender.

Before moving to the next step, ensure you have achieved some consistency in your ability to surrender and occasionally feel a light, positive energy during practice, which will grow in due course. Stay attuned to your inner body with every conscious breath, noticing the space and stillness that resides within. By distancing yourself from your body and mind and removing the narratives associated with your feelings, you'll find that suffering diminishes more swiftly and is transformed into peace over time.

"Such men are not only in concentration camps. Everywhere man is confronted with fate, with the chance of achieving something through his own suffering."

—Viktor E. Frankl,
Man's Search for Meaning

BODY SCAN MEDITAION

◇

Awareness in Death

Begin by arriving.

Let the body settle into stillness—either seated or lying down.
Let your breath come naturally, soft and unforced, as you comfortably slow it.

Close your eyes. Feel the ground beneath you. Feel the quiet presence within. (Reopen your eyes for reading, but keep them close as you progress in this meditation style)

Start with the breath.
No control—just notice. A few simple, honest breaths. Follow the rise and the fall. Feel the chest expand and release. Allow your body to relax as if you're beginning to disappear into the moment.

Now imagine this:
Death has arrived.
Not as pain, not fear, but *as silence*.
Not as dying, but to be dead.

Let the thought pass through you gently. The mind is gone. The chatter has stopped.
What remains?

A quiet awareness still holds...the faintest light... something still here, still sensing.
This is where we are.

Bring your awareness now to what remains—start with your hands. Feel the palms, the fingers, the sub-tle energy resting there. Then the back of the hands. Let the breath soften into every sensation. Take your time in each part.

Move to the forearms, elbows, and upper arms. Breathe through them slowly, as if light is *flowing* in with every inhale and *dissolving* tension with every exhale.

Let this breath climb to the shoulders—softening,

melting, loosening what has been held.

Now to the throat. Breathe into any tightness. Feel the breath pass through with no resistance. Relax the jaw. Let the skin of the face go slack, expressionless, unburdened.

Bring attention to the chest. Then down to the belly. Inhale. Exhale. Allow your awareness to settle here, like a feather, floating down to rest.

Now (at your pace, in the same fashion) downward through the hips, thighs, and knees. Breathe into the shins, feet, and all the way down to the toes. Then, gently trace your energy up the back of the legs and into the spine. Let each vertebra soften. Let the back relax and unfold, breathing energy into any knots. Travel upward until you reach the neck, scalp, and the crown of the head.

Your body is relaxed.
Your breath is steady.
Your awareness is vast.

Now...fade deeper.
Imagine, gently, that you're accepting death—not

with fear, but with grace. A quiet merging. Awareness meets awareness. Thought dissipates. Form dissolves.

There is no "you" here. No memory, no story. Only this field—open, endless, still.

Stay here. Let your body breathe in this vastness. Let your awareness rest without effort.

Be here.
—As long as you wish.

And when it feels time to return, do so slowly. Feel the weight of your body again. Let the breath be natural. But keep something of that stillness with you.

Take it into your day, not as an idea, but as a way of being.

Let the ego fall away where it's not needed. Embrace the expansive quiet of what remains.

This is the practice.
A rehearsal for release
A reminder of what never truly was and what never truly dies.

— STEP THREE —

FOCUSED ATTENTION

With presence, we expand into the eternal Absolute within. Learn to fully embrace the moment and bring heaven to earth. Through focus and never-ending surrender to the heart, we grow ever closer to that which is holy, to what is meant by "transcendence," until all reality becomes recognized, and the one knowledge that gives all meaning is known.

Give up the notion of time completely and see the landscape and horizon ahead as pure inspiration, the adventure awaiting, where that inkling to something beyond the senses moves past questions into experience. By training unaltered acceptance of the one fluid moment, you become one with what is within. This is a discovery that can only be experienced; no amount of words will suffice, no amount of church will bring you where you must go alone. This moment is where the kingdom is, and others can point the way, but nobody can hold your hand through the door.

To transcend completely is to transcend more than just the mind. It's to move beyond sensual pleasure, and unmanifest the manifested. It's not to become just another animal; it's to become completely aware of the human potential. We're transcending into our senses. Observation, at its core, is the act of focusing fully on reality, free from all distractions. The more consistently you can hold this focus, without getting lost in thought, the closer you are to an effortless state of being. With practice, this awareness becomes second nature, enabling you to confront suffering head-on and deepen your commitment to mindfulness. This step marks a pivotal point in your spiritual journey, reinforcing the foundation for a truly present and conscious existence.

Mindfulness cannot remain a sporadic practice or reserved for meditation alone; it must become a constant staple throughout your daily life. Observe how long you can hold the 'mental gaps'—those moments of pure presence without thought, which can serve as an influential gauge of your growth (as also famously pointed out by Ramana Maharshi). Let the sense of inner awareness permeate into everything you do, whether it's casual conversations or more mentally demanding tasks. While a simple meditation is beneficial for stress relief and growth, consistent presence enables the alleviation of conceptualized fear in every situation, creating a deeper, more lasting transformation. Aim for a continuous flow of practice, integrated naturally into your routine.

In this step, your observations focus on three areas: the body, visual perception, and auditory experiences. These are the anchors for your awareness. So far, the observative practice has primarily centered on taking the mind inward, refining the ability to 'watch and wait' as the foundation for clarity, then focusing on your emotional presence for growth. Now, mastering unwavering focus will extend that practice, giving surrender space to yield significant results. It's time to not just practice presence, but to *live* it—letting the surface layers of self dissolve into the ever-expanding gaps of absolute awareness.

To maintain your focus and prevent monotony, alternate between different types of observations as needed. The practice from step two—going inward to feel the presence of your inner body—should always be paired with these external observations, forming a dynamic loop of inner and outer awareness. Over time, this blending of practices will become seamless; for now, feel free to alternate as you grow more comfortable and at ease. Throughout this step, I'll share examples from my own life where each type of observation deepened my connection to the moment. However, first, let's discuss objectivity.

To be Objective

For millennia, philosophers have wrestled with the question, "What is truth?" These arguments often revolve around abstract definitions or debates about metaphorical interpretations or terminology. While these discussions have their place, they can feel removed from lived experience. What if, instead of always asking questions like these, we turned the questioning toward a more practical and relative perspective, with an emphasis on the variability of objectivity itself? What does it mean to be objective? To what degree is objectivity possible? Is thinking a requirement of objectivity? And also: what happens when we observe reality directly (in the style this book seems to suggest)?

Too often, the idea of truth becomes tangled in subjective values or confused with what might be called "objective subjectivity," where facts are interpreted through the lens of the subject. What I argue is this: the "subject" itself can be entirely dropped (and this is not catastrophic), and this deserves personal experimentation. Beyond the strong opinions and facts filtered through the mind, there is reality as it absolutely is. In this state, the one truth reveals itself—the same truth any metaphor or paradox points to—not as a construct of thought but as a direct individual experience of being.

Is pure objectivity possible? Pure, true objectivity is not only possible—it is transformative. It aligns with the highest level of spirituality, where presence is effortless, and thoughts arise only when explicitly needed. This kind of objectivity is rare, not because it is unattainable, but because few are willing to commit to the practice that would lead to it. It requires inward courage to step beyond the comfort of familiar patterns, and even more to sustain the pursuit until reaching its epoch. Those who do experience life with unparalleled clarity and feel what it is to be a spirit. To deny the possibility of pure objectivity is to deny the legitimacy of people such as Eckhart Tolle, Ramana Maharshi, the Buddha, and even (probably) Jesus Christ. Assuming every person who reaches the acme of spirituality is a liar is an assumption that can only be made without any experiential effort. However, if effort were to be made, it would take an authentic attempt in good faith—the kind of effort (at least a modicum of) the sages themselves put into it.

At the opposite end of the spectrum, the lowest degree of objectivity is often accompanied by heightened negative emotions or erratic emotional states, encompassing a pendulum of mania and impulsivity, or it can simply be complete self-absorption. In these states, the mind generates an overwhelming torrent of thoughts, distorting perceptions and clarity. Mindfulness can be a useful remedy here, helping to ground the mind through focused awareness and presence. Many people invariably know to some extent how to practice mindfulness, such as taking mental breaks while thinking, or having a knack for letting thoughts flow, or taking a breath before a stressful situation. If these types of techniques do not come naturally, they are useful to learn, and there is plenty of material available on these topics. These states can also be improved through small adjustments, such as maintaining a better sleep schedule and a healthier diet. That being said, to pretend it isn't possible or desirable to fully embrace this type of objectivity, when it is and has always been recommended to any varying degree, is simply an attachment to the mind and its need to fortify its usefulness.

For most of us, thinking feels indispensable—it's how we solve problems, make decisions, and interpret the world. But is it completely necessary?

Surprisingly, much of our surface-level thinking—self-talk, imagined scenarios, and compulsive analysis—is not only unnecessary but can actively hinder our ability to perceive the world clearly.

The deeper mind, however, operates through stored knowledge and quick intuition. It recognizes patterns and processes information at a level beyond words. This unconscious ability requires far less mental construction than we may realize. While thinking is a powerful tool and should be treated as such, it's not the sole—or even primary—path to understanding truth. True objectivity, then, is less about constructing mental frameworks and more about dissolving them, allowing reality to reveal itself unfiltered.

As you extend the intervals of mental quiet, something remarkable happens: your inner spirit begins to shine through, unobscured by the mind's chatter. This quietness allows a deeper understanding of life to emerge—one that is not built on conceptual judgment but on direct experience. In this state, clarity flows naturally, unburdened by mental effort. Thoughts become tools—used purposefully for problem-solving, creativity, or communication, rather than incessant intrusions.

I'll also point out that in this state, when thinking, words come out much more like whispers of their former selves, with much less visual imagination, and both become exceptionally reluctant to be evoked. Actions become more authentic, driven by peace or inspiration rather than a need for specific outcomes. Superficial desires fall away, leaving room for a singular, unshakable meaning to guide your life. Emotions get seen for what they are, augmentable and changeable, simply distortions of reality. Emotions seem to melt back into one, and in doing so, the ego simultaneously joins in on this "returning to the root," through the process of surrender. In general, you operate on a more parasympathetic level, growing in consciousness as a result of less thinking.

I don't recommend that thinking itself shouldn't be cultivated or that the ego is useless; it's only a part of the extended nature of humanity. I personally wouldn't recommend this high level of objective awareness until after the age of thirty, and even if the highest state is reached, considering a return to a level of ego might be desirable, perhaps to follow a purpose or spread wisdom. I say this because youth and the mind should be allowed to run their course; after all, you have to live in society, and there is no transcendence without mental development. As for returning to a state of ego, that is simply a personal choice in a given situation, and the experience and knowledge you gain will stay with you forever.

Letting go of habitual thinking brings clarity, authenticity, and a profound connection to existence itself. Truth, in this stillness, is no longer something to be sought or dissected—it simply is. In the silence of the mind and body, you come face to face with the root of all things. In observing and knowing this root, you come to know yourself.

Bodily Observation

To truly live is to directly experience life as it is at its source. Perceiving the physical senses of the body helps you connect with the most fundamental aspect of existence—awareness in its purest, most embodied form. This practice is a doorway to understanding what spirit is, the very essence that animates all life, the all-pervading energy that gives meaning and awareness to the universe.

To observe the body is to tune into the energy and sensations of the specific parts of your form—whether it's your hands, feet, back, or even your hamstrings. Similar to the body scanning meditation, you focus on one area at a time and become acutely aware of all the sensations it holds. This could be the energy radiating from or within that part, the texture of an object you're touching, the temperature nearby, or even the subtle feelings of fatigue or itchiness.

Try combining the sensation of touch with the act of noticing the energy within the body. For example, while typing, feel the keys of the keyboard and simultaneously sense the energy in your fingers (as I might be doing now). Allow your attention to shift completely to that part of the body. To deepen awareness, breathe into the area of focus. If you're sensing your fingertips, take a slow, deep breath in, and as you exhale, let that awareness expand to your whole hand, following the rhythm of your breath. As you continue, try to see if you can feel this awareness expanding further and further, eventually encompassing the entirety of your body. This technique, in its root form of inner expansion, works well in all areas of mindfulness practice.

To help expand awareness, you can also begin to shift your awareness to a more subtle layer— become aware of awareness itself. Who is feeling these sensations? Who is observing them? This is a practice of observing the observer, to recognize that the awareness behind these sensations is not separate from the essence of your being. It deepens the practice of body perception into a spiritual inquiry, helping dissolve the illusion of separation between you and the energy within.

A great time to practice this technique is during routine activities that might typically lead to mind wandering, such as eating, showering, or doing an easy task. A popular example is when showering, or maybe swimming, focus on the sensation of water on your skin—its temperature, and any tingling or shifting sensations—and as thoughts arise, gently let them go and return to the feeling of the water. You can even practice various techniques during a haircut or while waiting for your food. Maybe you're opening a door, notice the knob as it turns, and all the physical sensations associated with it. These moments, though often mindless, present an opportunity for a light and simple meditative practice, with an increasing habit of focus while performing automated actions.

Daily life offers endless opportunities to perceive the body, whether it's noticing the texture of an object you're handling or the internal energy of any part of the body. By consistently integrating this practice into your daily routine, you enhance your mindfulness and gradually help eliminate negative habits.

Body perception serves as a bridge between the physical and the spiritual. By tuning into the subtle sensations of the body, you tap into the flow of your lifeforce, which often goes unnoticed during the hustle of daily existence. These sensations are more than surface-level experiences—they're pathways that lead you to a deeper understanding of your body as a vessel of energy and awareness. If you focus and expand your awareness on the sensations, you'll notice that you're tuning into the flow of life's energy itself.

The transformative power of this observing technique lies in its connection to the inner senses and in strengthening our awareness of what's happening within, as well as in its relation to surrender. It roots us in the moment, shifting focus from the mind to the body, interrupting the cycle of habitual thinking that usually dominates our attention. In those moments of full awareness, the mind's chatter fades, and we experience the stillness within that allows us to connect with a deeper part of ourselves. This connection to the present moment lays the groundwork for genuine transformation. By staying in touch with the body, we become naturally more aligned with our authentic self, breaking free from the ego's hold.

I've often spent the first part of my meditations focused on the energy in the inner torso, breathing into that space, showing how closely I relate it to surrender. On walks to my car at work, I would gradually become aware of my feet as I walked, while maintaining visual focus on my surroundings. Once in the car, it would grow into full-body awareness, with eyes closed, and deepen and expand into inner awareness until time seemed to stop completely, turning ten-minute breaks into what sometimes felt like hours.

Body sensing, like any practice, takes time to master. Initially, you may only be able to focus on one part of the body until your mind starts to wander. That's okay. With consistent practice, you'll find that your ability to stay present with your body will naturally grow. Over time, you may even notice a light, emanating awareness of your entire body at once, fully connected to your physical form without the need to focus on a particular part—a sign that your presence is deepening, and your mind is becoming less dominant. In more profound moments, you may experience an intense explosion of this inner awareness (what I might call energetic rapture). For me, this often occurred during the process outlined in step four, which will be discussed again.

Remember, this practice is not about perfection but presence. Every moment spent in awareness of the body is a step toward deeper clarity and peace. Be patient with yourself as you learn to expand your awareness and surrender the mental noise. With time, body sensing will become second nature, and you'll find yourself more present, more connected, and more in tune with the energy that flows through all things.

Visual Observation

Separate yourself from nature to become one with who you are. This paradox exists only because of the belief that you are your mind. While it's a valuable spiritual practice to see yourself in all things (which we will discuss), there is another layer to observing reality. Instead of seeing yourself as just another part of the scenery, try viewing the objects around you as existing solely for your observation, free from mental attachments to stories and judgments.

Only humans believe we're a part of nature; the rest of nature simply is. No animal sees you and is confused about the boundary between itself and the object in front of it. Through mental absorption, what we see becomes an extension of our mentality. Surrender and embrace clarity. Become the pure observer, understanding that the world exists for your awareness, not for your judgment. Though you're destined to be "in the world," as Jesus said in the gospels, you're not required to be "of it."

Visual observation could be the most intuitive form of mindfulness, likely due to the direct link between awareness and eyesight. If you were to imagine present-moment awareness, it might resemble observing your surroundings as if seeing them for the first time, free from thoughts or labels. When we attach labels, everything we see gets unconsciously filtered through the mind's judgment parameter, carrying with it all the values and previous verdicts the ego has assigned.

In practice, this means looking at each object without attaching any mental commentary—seeing it as it is, not as your mind defines it. You take notice of the simple presence of things, eliminating the need for context or judgment, which only exist in thought. When you observe in this way, even the most mundane objects can suddenly appear vivid and beautiful. It's incredible how our inner narrative colors our perception, and how different the world feels when the narrative is absent.

If you find it challenging to maintain visual focus without labels, try imagining that you're simply vision itself, as if everything behind your eyes (your head) has faded into air. Although I didn't use this technique directly during the height of my practice, I've since seen similar ideas recommended. In my experience, this lightness of mind was present more unconsciously and undoubtedly aided my focus. Projecting this "light" feeling can bring a sense of weightlessness, an ease of focus that can enhance mental clarity and skill. Allow yourself to dissolve into the space around you.

All forms exist within space; without space, there would be no objects to be held. As you observe, allow yourself to become aware of the space around and between things, noticing how much of everything is this "emptiness." Space is not just outside of you but also within you—the same emptiness exists between the particles that make up your body. There is substance in this emptiness. The Absolute pervades all, including what lies in between forms. *Soften your gaze*, appreciating the vastness that holds all things in place, and in doing so, become aware of the deeper connection between all things.

One of my favorite ways to practice visual observation is while driving. Initially, being in high presence while driving might feel unusual—even nerve-racking—but you'll soon discover that it can make driving less stressful, not more. You'll notice how your mind typically labels everything around you: the cars, the road signs, annoying fellow travelers, even the trees passing by. Start by simply paying attention to these things without labeling or judging them, while of course, staying safely focused on the road. At stoplights, take the opportunity to deepen your stillness—perfect moments for a short meditation. This practice turns a routine activity into a rewarding mindfulness exercise. Mindfulness isn't limited to tranquil settings alone, and it shouldn't be. Embrace the challenge, and practice surrender in those moments of useless irritation.

As a caveat: if you feel like mindfulness practice is distracting or too challenging while driving, prioritize safety and pause the practice until you feel comfortable.

Try applying this practice at work as well. While performing tasks that don't require deep thought (again, while staying safe), observe your surroundings, including the space around you, and let go of unnecessary mental commentary. Allow yourself to flow through a task without the usual mental commentary. You don't have to disengage completely when performing tasks that require mental engagement, but you'll be surprised how much you can achieve without compulsive thinking. On a more philosophical note, by also not labeling tasks as stressful or tedious, you can increase your focus and productivity without the mental burden that usually accompanies them. In general, your stress will lessen, and the relief you gain from an easier work life will positively affect everything you do.

When observing the objects and space around you, it may help to continually refocus on different objects or points in space. Notice when your mind tries to add narratives, and become aware of the timing, redirecting your attention before it gets pulled into thought. Different levels of general energy—related to diet, rest, and overall health—might affect your need to shift focus, as well as your current spiritual state, both of which will reverberate into everything you do. However, do what you can at any given state and adjust accordingly—more wakefulness will have a positive impact on your life.

My favorite personal philosophy here has always been what I've read from Lao Tzu: to "soften your gaze." This soft gaze helps keep focus light and open, especially when directing it toward space itself. Besides shifting your focus on objects, you may also alternate between an intense focus on objects and a softer gaze related more to space, and use whichever style feels more natural to you in that moment.

Let the light of consciousness shine through the visual sense. The eyes do more than absorb—they reflect the soul. Eyes undoubtedly reveal our inner life, from the pure empathy of the child to the inspiration of the hero and the liar alike. The spirit holds no judgment of the mind's content; it is the Absolute, the unmanifested. It sits in the shadows of judgments and fixations, waiting to emerge when the world is seen without filters, in pure, absolute reality.

Auditory Observation

Auditory focus opens a path to one of our most immediate senses—hearing. Sound is always around us, yet most of it is obscured in the background. In practicing auditory mindfulness, we learn to truly listen. By turning attention to the sounds surrounding us, we create a gateway to deeper presence and connect with a stillness that lies beneath the noise of daily life. This practice is more than just listening to sounds; it's about embracing the quiet spaces within and around us, discovering a deeper clarity, and accessing the peace that silence offers.

Whenever you find yourself at a standstill, take the opportunity to focus intently on the sounds around you. Clear your mind and begin by isolating a single sound that stands out. Let this pause be an opportunity to practice attentive listening, as if you were trying to hear a conversation on the other side of the door. Lightly see if that single sound can increase in intensity and become audible above all other noise.

Once you've tuned in to a prominent sound, try shifting your attention to background noises you hadn't noticed before. You might hear the hum of machinery, a distant airplane, or a rustle in a bush. Hear the different layers of sounds as well, and pay attention to their combinations. How does one sound stand out more than another? To what degree? Notice the texture or hardness, or lack thereof. Is the sound sharp or soft? Notice these things without outright thinking. Whatever the sound may be, this heightened awareness can demonstrate the effectiveness of your senses when your mind isn't cluttered with thoughts.

Beyond individual sounds, there is the silence underlying them. This silence is there amongst all the noise. Listen closely and stay with it; there is little more spiritual than the sound of silence. Listen to the space between words in conversations. Focus on the quiet between that humming noise somewhere nearby and the singing bird outside the window. Hear what is too often forgotten, the silence in the space.

Take the silence even deeper and listen *inward*. Shift your focus to what lies within the body, listening for the stillness within. Give attention to the quiet at your core, then expand that inner silence as if dropping into an endless void. The more you tune into silence, the more you'll find peace. Silence is the language of the Divine, it invites us to rest in what is, beyond mental noise.

During meditation, relax with your eyes closed, listen to what surrounds you, and progressively drift into silence. Then, gradually bring the quiet within, all the while allowing yourself to dissipate with the flow of energy and breath. When silence and surrender become one, you become one. This is how you hear true wisdom, the easiest path to correct knowledge and pure observation. If this is done at the beginning of any meditation, no matter the type, all immediate meditation and practice thereafter will be done in its fullest. This is my favorite way to begin all my meditations, which can last anywhere from a few minutes to the entire sitting.

When you observe others through auditory (and see from visual) awareness, free from labels, memories, and assumptions, you respect them as their true inner being. By not defining others by their past actions or personality traits, you offer them your purest attention and free yourself from the weight of preconceived notions. Even when someone has hurt or wronged you, seeing them through the lens of presence diminishes their influence, allowing you to interact with them without stress or avoidance.

Embrace auditory focus to become the attentive listener heralded in all discussions on effective communication. Focused listening enables you to give others your undivided attention, resulting in more authentic interactions. This method enables you to respond promptly and clearly without over occupying yourself with what to say next while the other person is speaking. Practice applying auditory focus whenever you're engaged in a conversation, and remember to focus more on what the other person is saying; an added benefit is that it won't be necessary to actively try to clear your mind while focused on someone else's words.

As you consistently listen in this manner, you might notice how much others enjoy speaking with you and want your company. With ongoing practice, you'll find yourself more relaxed and able to mentally jot down key points, enhancing your ability to respond thoughtfully and accurately. Your responses will grow more considerate and impactful, carrying confidence without aggression. This improvement can benefit not only your professional and family life, but also enhance all areas of interpersonal communication.

You may notice that at times, when entering the auditory observation, an incredible amount of noise suddenly drops off, and you zone in, almost as if there's an entire shift in the way your awareness operates, as the white noise of the mind falls away. This demonstrates how easily we can become detached from the present moment and the drastic shift that is possible when we focus.

Additionally, we learn that the incessant background thoughts and automatic labeling of everything around us are not integral parts of who we are. Snap back into reality as often as possible, recognizing that what you previously feared and considered "reality" was just a continuous cycle of noise morphing into daydreams and nightmares. Confront any regret and apprehension by embracing what is real, focusing purely and objectively.

Entire books and teachings are devoted to the practice of focused listening. If auditory focus resonates with you, I encourage you to dedicate more time to it, both in meditation and throughout your daily activities. Also, if any particular aspect of the practice suits you well, let it guide you, using other techniques as supplements. However, try to gain a comprehensive understanding of all teachings and ensure you don't overlook any part of your practice.

Incorporate this practice throughout your day, not just during moments of stillness. When walking, listen to the birds or the rustling of the wind. At work, be aware of your fingers typing, the sound of machinery, or even the sound of your footsteps. Blend this auditory focus with visual observation to achieve a deeper sense of relief or to introduce a fresh element to your ongoing presence. Enjoy this practice and let silence become a consistent theme in your life, maintaining it as an integral part of your being.

In a world where sound and the mind continually drown out silence, the auditory sense is a bridge to inner peace. By tuning into both sounds and the silence around us, we strip away the layers of distraction and come closer to experiencing life as it is. Each moment of pure attention brings us closer to our higher self, unencumbered by mental noise. Through attentive listening, we not only enrich our relationships with others but also deepen our relationship with the world around us. As we embrace silence more fully, we discover a sanctuary of calm that we can carry into every aspect of our lives—a calm that requires no words, only presence.

Integrating Steps in Observation Practice

Remember to integrate the foundational steps as you deepen your observational practice. Begin with a few conscious breaths, which can center you and create some easy mental space, allowing you to step out of habitual thought patterns. Once grounded, turn your mind inward, focusing on the heart center or lower abdomen (or wherever your spiritual epicenter may be). From there, engage in the act of observation, directing your attention outward toward the details of your surroundings.

Observation itself doesn't have to be the final step in this process; it can be the starting point. By focusing on your environment first, you may find it easier to then move inward, and perhaps breathe consciously, allowing you to feel the energy in your body. Observing your surroundings can provide an anchor for your awareness, gently diverting attention away from mental noise and back into the present moment.

Nature walks, or any walks for that matter, are ideal opportunities for practicing all forms of observation. They serve as a form of moving meditation, allowing you to engage in mindfulness without the distractions often present in daily life. As you walk, observe the scenery around you—the swaying trees, the sky, the way the light filters through the leaves. Listen to the sounds that surround you. Feel the sensation of your feet meeting and leaving the ground, noticing the rhythm of each step. Simultaneously, you can delve inward (again, of course), attuning to the energy within.

This multifaceted engagement not only enhances your awareness but also enriches the experience itself. The aim is to move through the steps of this book fluidly, allowing each component to support and deepen the others. Over time, this layered approach to observation will become more intuitive, bringing a greater sense of unity between inner awareness and outer presence.

Boredom

What might be called boredom, for many, is a serious obstacle, distinguished by a need to self-distract. If this is the case, become comfortable with boredom and move through it with a sense of surrender. Accept it and realize it's not that bad after it settles in. If you look at others who seem to progress better, in whatever manner, they seem particularly more apt at handling boredom and distractions. Leaning into boredom, with a sense of "powering through" to some degree, will open doors in your life and give real inspiration room to flourish.

This will naturally become easier as you become more proficient in presence, blossoming with time as you habituate spiritual practice. It's found in the ability to work with silence (not against it), without needing distraction. This is essentially training focus—the purest way of doing so—through unadulterated objective attention.

Attention and Gratitude

In today's world, many of us have become more addicted to receiving attention than giving it.

This trend manifests in various ways, including emotional outbursts, a preference for speaking rather than listening, and taking unhealthy shortcuts in our appearance. Often, when we encounter such behavior, it evokes a sense of discomfort—a certain ickiness that's hard to pinpoint, but might stem from a perceived lack of effort, honesty, and authenticity. It feels like a shallow craving for attention rather than a deep-seated desire to be genuinely appreciated.

There is a distinct difference between seeking attention and earning appreciation. Attention seekers aim to be seen, often regardless of the substance behind their actions. This can be profitable and provide worthwhile comforts, but whether it reaches any ideal of fulfillment is up for debate. In contrast, those who are truly appreciated engage deeply in the moment, driven by inspiration and creativity. They represent an underlying principle, something beyond concept—soul. We celebrate these individuals—some of whom are indeed sages—because they embody and capture profound moments that leave a lasting impact, through the act of appreciation itself. They earn undying appreciation out of respect for the life they have given.

To harness your moment, embody that sense of appreciation. Let it rise into all your observations.

Feel the essence of gratitude even when it seems there is little to appreciate. Observe your surroundings and allow yourself to feel grateful. This practice may seem challenging or frivolous at first and may be easily resisted, but it is more attainable and valuable than it appears. Imagine what it feels like to live with undying gratefulness and aim to embody this feeling as frequently as possible. Become like the great sage, wholly present and appreciative of each moment.

The way I use the terms "appreciation" and "gratitude" is an attempt to capture the essence of unconditional love, or a joyous inner light free from labels. Other substitutable terms include prudence, meaning, connection, or pure attention. The form of appreciation I describe doesn't absorb and abstract mentally, but instead radiates from within. This selfless attention fulfills a fundamental human desire beyond mere survival and thriving—it meets our deep need for connectivity, simply by turning the means into the end itself. Thus, appreciation is one of the most significant gifts you can offer someone in any situation, and it is also the greatest gift you can give yourself, aligning closely with life's greatest purpose: being conscious of consciosness.

The constant grasping, clinging, and dwelling on desires leads to misery, driven by an unfulfilled need exacerbated by mental preoccupation. A fulfilled being, however, radiates from the heart without expecting anything in return. This person experiences continual joy, understanding that a quiet mind welcomes no troubles, and an open heart excludes no one. This is the essence of spirit. Whether you refer to it as the higher self or simply a state of gratitude, recognize that being grateful is always possible.

Let appreciation become your prevailing state, feeling peace within your heart. As you breathe into this feeling, discover the breadth of what this state can offer. Engage in this growing appreciation while practicing any of the observations mentioned earlier. Doing so will elevate your spiritual energy and enhance the joy in both your life and practice. It will help sharpen your focus, significantly reduce your inclination toward negativity, and increase your openness to creativity and meaningful action.

Observing God in Everything

You might find that when you look deeply, desires, values, and motives all point toward something whole and unifying—what can be called the Absolute, consciousness, or simply a state of everlasting inner peace. Other names for this concept include fulfillment, wholeness, the Tao, Holy Spirit, Brahma, Dharma, and many others (in step two, the term "bliss" was used). This is the primal source of all creation. Being fully in sync with this consciousness is where true fulfillment lies.

What's more, the purpose for *why* we do anything is one and the same as *who* we are. The basic drive to survive and replicate, while fundamental to our existence, isn't enough on its own. That original spark—life, energy aware of itself—is consciousness, and consciousness is of peace, not of fear or mind. Without this connection to life, survival instincts become distorted with the ego involved, leading to strange, manipulative, and even destructive behaviors that defy the purpose of survival itself.

We're graced, or at least many of us are, by our guardians with an internal connection, from the utero on out through development. There may be no statement truer than that "God is a mother's embrace." She not only gives birth, but also instills life. Empathy is a gift, and though the Absolute may reside in all, it may be forever obscured by the mind built on fear alone. As guardians to our children, it's our duty not only to prepare them for the world, but also to pass on the connection to life itself.

It's not that consciousness is developed; rather, it's the task of parents to establish the connection to consciousness. Though a well-nurtured intellect is highly desirable, an empathetic connection to life is the parent's foremost responsibility. It's the value we all (or most of us) naturally look for in others, and in how others instill it in their young; a value no one can help but gravitate toward. There is, of course, the smooth transition away from this original dependence for individuality and fortitude, but nothing else has a greater impact on life than the *connection* to life.

Without an internalized, loving connection in the formative years, the ego is vulnerable to becoming severely disturbed, or in a lesser degree generally desperate; the former resulting in the more dangerous aspects that torment a society, the latter being the more general and seemingly salvageable result, manifesting in the direction of egotistical and neurotic behaviors (self-absorption). These self-absorbed, or desperate, behaviors are often an overcompensation for a lack of connection, with the ego constantly seeking to fill the void. In my view, if the ego can be either augmented by discipline or eliminated through spirituality, and if the ego can be destructive in almost any environment, then this connected sense of the whole is, above all, necessary for existence and its survival.

Empathy is not only an outward projection, but also an inward connection; without this *care* it's not just carelessness for others, there is a lacking sense of consequences to the self—either in the egotistical inability to see how our self and actions are creating constant volatile situations and relationships, or as seen in full in the extreme forms of sociopathology. Without connection, destruction lies in the wake, and to begin with, life wouldn't propagate at all.

Though experiences shape us at every stage of life, the ultimate purpose throughout life and in its lessons remains constant: to reconnect with our authentic selves and find inner fulfillment. Philosophers excel in analyzing and categorizing reality, breaking it into recognizable value systems that help us understand the world intellectually. However, this understanding is incomplete without action. While philosophical discussions will often circle an idea that all the "whys" lead to one end, an end I clearly see as fulfillment, they often stop at talk. An overarching theme in philosophy and value is (as my simple generic example): take any object, like a plate or a bike, and if you keep asking why you use them, and ask "why" again to every response, the answer eventually distills into the feeling of fulfillment, God or the (universal) Absolute at the base for everything. Although this finding is an incredible discovery, one that everyone should acknowledge, spirituality extends beyond mere talk in this regard. It walks the path of experience, recognizing and *embodying* that great answer of fulfillment that so much philosophy only describes.

A fundamental misstep is not acknowledging the fleeting nature of attachment in all its forms, and that the root feeling that drives all thought, actions, and emotions can become consistently realized with practice. That feeling is one of being our true selves, through the unification of value and meaning. This knowledge—fully comprehended and with constant internal validation—goes beyond discussion. What's more, regarding the more spiritual or religious aspect of humanity, to continually experience this knowledge is the prerequisite to expanding past mere religious belief in God; it's to know God.

In practice, this means seeing and feeling the Absolute in every person, every experience, and every moment. Once you see that everything is connected to this root, you can skip the layers of superficial values and treat all as an expression of this Divine essence. This awareness, held tight, will fortify the mindful way you interact with others, as it's not only your purpose but the underlying purpose of anyone you encounter.

Seeing God in everything is a cornerstone of nearly all spiritually centered paths, from the Dharma practice of Buddhism to the Tao of Taoism, and also in the teachings of the Upanishads and Vedas—terms like prana, Dharma, and the Tao refer to that ultimate value discussed. Strengthening this view will elevate your practice, amplify your inner light, and allow mindfulness to transcend into spirituality.

Practice recognizing this deeper essence in all observational practice, in every moment, and acknowledge the presence of absolute consciousness. Blend that appreciation, gratitude, and inspiration, all of which mean the same as the inner light and holiness, stepping back and letting this attention shine through. Holding this objectivity will transform your life, allowing everything you observe to reflect the beauty and connection of the Absolute.

Recap

This journey is about expanding your awareness, instilling stillness, and embracing the present moment in all its beauty. Allow space to feel infinite, without a center or edge, and notice its lightness. Let silence be an ongoing void, impenetrable and ever-present.

Allow the inner light to flow through you, embracing appreciation as your constant state of being, with the heart as the seat of consciousness.

We outlined the three primary modes of perception—bodily, visual, and auditory senses. Starting with the body: feel your energy from within and always expand your awareness in this way. Engage with the objects around you; touch them and experience their texture. Sense all externally and internally. Throughout the day, bring your attention to different parts of your physical form, such as your hands, feet, and even your entire body. This practice sharpens sensory awareness and helps in identifying emotional locations and specific feelings, which can benefit surrender.

From the sensations of your body, shift to the world around you. Use your eyes for their most natural purpose—observation. Look at your surroundings without constructions of time, as if seeing everything for the first time. Appreciate the effort it takes to maintain this perspective and how it can clear the mind. Notice the space around you, recognizing its vastness, and know that same vastness exists within you.

Now, listen closely to the sounds in your environment, moving your focus from one sound to the other. Be aware of the underlying silence that frames these sounds and listen for the silence within your own body, finding peace in its depth. Silence is not merely the absence of noise; it is the presence of stillness—the language of the Absolute, the soul.

Feel gratitude while engaging in your observations. Embrace it as you delve into the inner workings of your body, and pair it with the tranquility that emanates from the heart. Experience the fullness of being in a complete state of gratitude, making this your preferred way of being at all times. From this state, observe your surroundings without the clutter of mental commentary or narratives, enabling a state of acceptance facilitated by unwavering prudence and meaning.

Be flexible with your focus, alternating between different observational practices as feels right in the moment. Whether it's visual, auditory, or bodily senses, stick with whichever keeps you present the longest, most often, and most rapidly. Feel free to flow between methods or change them as needed, choosing what feels most comfortable and effective at that time.

I often like to mix elements from the first three steps as a way to keep the practice fresh and spontaneous. Typically, I start by observing the mind, then take a slow, conscious breath inward and transition into a state of observation. Repeating this cycle a few times usually results in the observations becoming more dominant and stable, less prone to interruption. You don't need to scrutinize every thought as you might in step one, unless it's necessary; the goal is to maintain a clear mind and give way to surrender.

Ultimately, this practice is about reconnecting to yourself at its root—a state of clarity, unity, and stillness that resides within you. By weaving presence into your daily life, you create a space for profound transformation and deeper connection to the world around you. Fear diminishes, gratitude flows, and the craving for external attention dissolves when you are attention itself. Observe the Absolute in all, and within.

"To the mind that is still, the whole universe surrenders."

—Lao Tzu,
Tao Te Ching, chapter 16

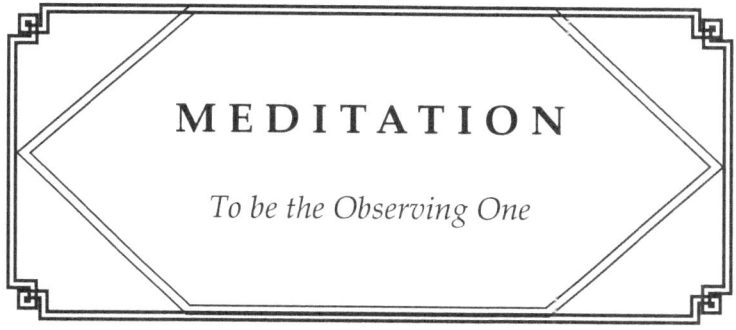

MEDITATION

To be the Observing One

Begin by softening into stillness.

Let your breath slow—not by force, but by release.
Breathe into separation, observing the world from
outside it. The body grows quiet. The mind settles.

This is not just about relaxation; it's about shedding
all assumptions and doubts. You're no longer the
thinker, the doer. You're the witness.

Let awareness sink into the body.

Begin wherever attention is drawn. Perhaps the hands,
or the face, or maybe within the chest. Rest there
fully. Feel that place from within. Let that awareness
expand—as if you're not just sensing, but *becoming*
the sensation itself.

Then move deeper.

Feel the still point behind all of it.
The seat of consciousness.

Feel the depth here—the silence, the clarity, the power
in stillness. It doesn't need to act. It sees. It holds. It
knows. Allow yourself to sink deeper into this center,
as if falling into a vast, infinite darkness.

And now, accept this truth:

This is the Absolute.

Not a distant deity, but the clear field of consciousness
from which all things arise.

There is no resistance. This essence doesn't crave. It
doesn't judge.
It simply *is*. And it is *you*.

Now, begin hearing.

Listen—not as your small self, but as divinity.
Hear what is nearby. Hear what is far. Don't name or

evaluate.

Listen as omniscience—pure, still, neutral attention.
Let each sound arise and drift with perfect allowance.

If your mind wanders, return to the sound or find a
new sound to give attention to.
Let it rest in your awareness.

Then listen for what is underneath, between, and
above the sound.
The vastness. The silence around the noise. The space
in which the sound floats.

Keep clear attention.

Let yourself see as an all-seeing being would see, as
God, not through thought, but through stillness.
Gaze upon the first object your attention lands on, like
aimlessly throwing a dart. Don't name it. Don't derive
it from yourself.

Breathe into it. Feel its essence. Focus with complete
intensity. Let your awareness burn hot with precision.

In this stage, thoughts may easily rise; if they do,
quickly give attention to another object, with the same

resounding intensity, breathing focus into it.

Stay fluid, and if labels arise, shift again.

Now, look not just at the object, but see the emptiness that it sits in. Just like with the sound, the space between everything. The invisible field holding all form.

This space is consciousness.
It's *your* consciousness—expansive, impersonal, indivisible.

Let yourself dissolve into this seeing.
You're separate, yet united. This is your gift.

Return to the center of the heart.
Breathe gently and slowly. Be stillness.

Let this meditation end not with effort, but with a sense of presence.
Close your eyes for a moment.
Carry it forward.

— S T E P F O U R —

The "I AM" Practice

"In the beginning there was the word," as was said, in Genesis of the Bible. With the word comes sentience, the bridge to meaning and spirit. Through the greatness of human inspiration and empathy comes this communicative possibility, and through our phonic ability comes the opportunity to acquire knowledge that sets a special place for us atop the animal kingdom. And so, the human steps beyond instincts alone. Not only because of the word, but because of the *possibility* of the word. With this possibility, all else becomes possible, and all belief realizable, from science back into the ecstasy of life, graced by such a unifying quality as the human spirit.

This unifying energy, as mentioned before, seeks to continually be aware of itself in the root knowledge of bliss. We're all exceptionally capable vessels, whether it be due to the development of opposable thumbs or sheer neuron development, etc. Through this comes our language, and along with it, the mind's underlying purpose to master survival.

There's no transcendence without the word. There's no religion, no guru, and no shamanistic rites and rituals dating back to prehistory. Without the word, neither science nor rationality could fully take shape. The spirit and reason are intertwined forever through the word, and bringing these two together is the person becoming a transcended and fulfilled individual.

If this is the case, then religion and all spirituality are the projection of language toward this goal, and science and rationality always seek after means, either consciously or unconsciously, toward the same outcome. Religion aims to know the soul, while science seeks to comfort the finite; both endeavors are valuable and part of the same, uniting process.

The Practice of "I Am"

Throughout a spiritual journey, you are bound to hear references to the phrase, "I am." At its essence, it's a clear affirmation through presence, and in the deepest sense, confirms, "I am God." The term "God" here is not confined to any particular religion but serves as a symbol for your highest self, you at the deepest level. It represents the aspect of you that observes everything with pure awareness, free from ego or judgment.

In this practice, we replace the noise of scattered thoughts with a singular, powerful affirmation that embodies who you really are. Over time, as other narratives fade away, this affirmation too dissolves. In this state, the chatter of the ego completely quiets, and the spirit shines through, leaving only pure presence and effortless being.

For me, my mantra became: "I am God. I am creative. And I am grateful." No one explicitly taught me these words, though there are plenty of suggestions out there on the "I am God" part. They arose naturally, through reflection and personal practice, and I found them to be profoundly effective. Whenever I spoke them deeply, as if sending them directly to the depths of my body, they graced me with unexplainable and inexhaustible waves of energy, or spirit. Inspired by the teachings that emphasized manifesting one's higher self and direct experience of absolute truth, I shaped my practices in a way that felt deeply authentic to me.

I had already developed the habit of clearing my mind and surrendering, so the use of a mantra naturally followed the lead of the processes outlined in the first three steps. Whenever I felt even the slightest pull of a thought—whether through mental chatter or through the urge to grasp at mental concepts—I'd take a conscious breath, center myself in the present, and repeat my mantra until my mind settled into stillness. Initially, I didn't recognize this as a "mantra practice." I simply followed what felt most effective for clearing my thoughts while encouraging self-knowledge.

You still don't fight your thoughts; instead, you allow them—and the desire to think—to naturally fade. The mantra serves as a gentle guide, leading you back to your center. Supplementing surrender involves releasing habitual pursuits, thoughts, and negative emotions. Over time, it grows in speed, and you let go instantly of the urge to grasp at mental noise, allowing presence to expand even further.

A Single Thought to End Thoughts

You're repeating your "I am" statement instead of all other thoughts, ceaselessly. The most popular statement, I assume, is "I am God" in its various forms, like "I am Brahmin," or one I would often use as a replacement or just add, "I am the Tao." The *Tao Te Ching,* by the sage Laozi, is personally one of my favorite spiritual teachings, taught through a clear, spiritual way of living, in the style of parable. The initial step is understanding and distinguishing your thoughts to realize your true essence and what is not; this ultimate step is knowing and embodying this essence, thereby completing the process and obliterating the need for personhood.

If you're like me, this may already be the case, but if you're serious about reaching a higher state of practice, I urge you to view thoughts as a danger (in a way), be on high alert, and return to the heart almost impatiently. From the happiest thoughts to the most depressing. Regardless of their nature, compulsive and conditioned thinking invariably leads to suffering. They foster personalities that are easily offended and reliant on external sources for satisfaction. Of course, there have been a lot of great memories, and there will be more; becoming present doesn't hinder this, and you cannot completely erase your past.

If you're in a constant state of despair, seeing it this way may not be too difficult. If not, know that in time thoughts become a nuisance, and even boring and repetitive; after all, you are reading this book for a reason, might as well see how far you can take it. As it turns out, there is so much more excitement when everything is experienced as new. It helps not to value one thought higher than the next, or more importantly, bundle them together as the source of too much irritation and let them float by. Even the thoughts with hefty emotions attached to them, when the smoke settles, this too was just another thought like all the rest.

You're trying to catch thoughts in the act at this point. You still shouldn't be forcing a thought out, but you should have the thought fade at a sooner and quicker rate. As the thought fades away or empties, repeat your mantra in a calm and comfortable manner. I would often do it on my exhale, echoing the words down into my body, while, in between these exhales, I would go back to complete, observant presence.

It might look like this: I take a deep breath, clearing my mind on the inhale, then on the exhale speak deeply within "I am God," then repeating the inhale style, and on the next exhale say, "I am creative," and then again in the same fashion, on the last exhale "I am Grateful." I would repeat my "mantra" several times (usually around three, equaling nine deep breaths), then work on presence practice with a silent mind. In time, the words you speak might grow quieter as you repeat and progress over the length of your practice, as if diminishing into a murmur in the background—this is natural.

If this practice proves too difficult, consider adjusting your approach, always with an attitude of allowing and letting go of doubt, and above all, returning within. Perfection isn't the goal here; consistency is. In my experience, this method has yielded significant results quickly, in harmony with the other steps described before. Although it may seem that this step isn't strictly necessary for achieving effortless awareness, I believe that focusing your thoughts on a single, beneficial mantra accelerates the process toward a clear mind, as you affirm your existence in the present— "I am," not "I will be."

By simplifying your mental activity to just one thought—a thought of virtue and wisdom—you facilitate its natural fading. This singular focus is easier to manage than a multitude of thoughts, and it's significantly easier than combating negative ones. Over time, practicing this focused thought will transform your mental imagery and narratives into mere observed whispers, and eventually, these whispers will quiet into silence.

It's important to emphasize that the first three steps prepare you for this practice. While mantras can be helpful at any stage of your journey, their full transformative power is unlocked after surrender and clarity have been honed. Without this foundation, words risk being filtered through the ego, where they are reduced to surface-level categorization and problem-solving. In an egoic state, the words fail to reach the deeper self.

When practiced in surrender, however, words take on profound resonance, bypassing the mind's automation and reaching the core of your being. They're no longer just words; they become a direct expression of presence.

This step, then, is not simply about repeating a mantra. It's about experiencing the transformative power of presence through a single, intentional affirmation—a mantra that reflects your highest self. As you let go of the ego's grasp, this practice becomes the culmination of your journey, clearing away the last remnants of mental noise and leaving you fully aligned with the truth of "I am."

I am God.

To say "I am God" is not to identify with thoughts or conditions, but to recognize the presence within—the part of you that exists beyond personal identity. This inner being is, in essence, undefinable and ethereal, but if the mind were to name it, it would be the source, the light of consciousness, the Absolute: God (use whatever term feels right to you, and note again, I consistently alternated the representing word).

Sometimes I would add extending phrases to this affirmation, like "I allow and I flow," and occasionally further, "I do not judge." While not necessary to the affirmation itself, these additions helped remind me how I defined God—how this higher self relates to the mind and body: as completely objective awareness and flowing, unifying energy.

God, as I've come to define it in relation to myself, as the Absolute, allows all conditions to exist and arise without resistance, accepting outcomes without clinging to the past or projecting into the future. The Absolute flows with life, not against it, and doesn't judge—for it's not bound to personality, nor to the fluctuating emotions of the ego. God is the mysterious presence, and that presence resides at the heart.

When I would speak the words "I am God," it often felt like energy from all around my being would gather into an ecstatic center, just at the bottom of my chest (where your breath within settles, the heart). It felt like the words were calling all spirit back to its root. This center held there, not in a strenuous way, but as if pointing me there as me, awaiting to be released.

I am creative.

I didn't always say "I am creative," at times simply sticking with just "I am God," and "I am grateful." This affirmation, in a way, was an ode to the type of mind I wanted to embody—fluid, expansive, and connected to spirit. If anything, it was my quick version of manifesting, as I would sometimes even add "I am a writer." When I spoke these words, I felt an energy ignite in my fingertips, aflame with spirit, as if consciousness as inspiration was extending out through my fingers.

This energy, unlike the feeling centered around the heart of "I am God," felt like it moved through the arms and hands into the fingers, toward expression. Creativity, as inspiration, is the outpouring of life through the mind and body. Whether that experience was purely symbolic or entirely physiological, I accepted it as part of the unfolding. This experience of energy did nothing to affect the energy that would be held from the previous affirmation.

I am Grateful.

The final statement released the energy that had been held since "I am God," plus some. Each time I spoke the words "I am grateful," the energy that had gathered in the body would rise and burst upward, out of the top of the head, as if gratitude were the completion of the circuit. It was the most intensely joyful sensation, like being lifted out as energy itself.

What's important to say is that I wasn't "grateful for" anything in particular. There was no conceptual reason attached to the feeling. It was simply the acknowledgment of gratitude itself as the correct mode of being, especially in light of the first two affirmations. It's to encompass gratitude. Gratitude for being, for the opportunity to know life, to be energy aware of itself, and the embracing of consciousness.

The Language of Spirit

These energetic experiences were just that— experiences. They happened seemingly non-stop throughout the day, whenever I would speak to them, and never lost luster. They're not superior to anything you've experienced, nor are they something to strive for. They were simply part of my path, and I followed them because they beckoned, but I cannot assume to know what beckons you.

While this occurred, I assure you I was skeptical of what was happening. I tried repeating the affirmations without any form of intent to see if they would still happen; it turns out that this often intensified the experience. I tried to go further, feeling as little as possible and being as mechanical as I could, but the words still held their power.

Eventually, I moved from speaking the words aloud to visualizing them. I would picture them as red cursive letters on a black background, and this seemed to retain the energetic effect, though to quite a lesser degree. Later, I let go of that image as well, in the pursuit of perfection (clarity was more valuable than rapture), and tried to feel the essence of the words, but the sensation weakened much further. Through this progression, one thing became clear: the spoken words themselves, in their concrete form, held a unique connection to the intensity of this experience.

In my view, this highlights the symbolic potency of language—the fact that certain words, especially when rooted in clear faith, can speak directly to something beneath the surface intention or thought. "I am" isn't just a phrase. It's a doorway.

Finishing Touches

As my practice deepened, I began to address residual narratives of the mind. Even after tackling dwelling, negative thoughts, and unnecessary mental commentary, I noticed that subtle narration persisted. This voice, though quieter, still created unnecessary noise. I recognized that these "helper thoughts," that seemed to guide or critique my practice and progress, were also still ego. They needed a little more than passive release—they needed to be actively dismissed (at the deeper stage, a more aggressive style becomes more plausible).

With practice, I replaced these residual thoughts with my mantra, but in a short time, even this began to feel unnecessary. As I mentioned, instead, I visualized the words in red cursive letters against a black background, allowing the image to naturally fade into presence. At the time, it astounded me how clear this image appeared, almost as if a stamp. No image has ever seemed more concrete in my mind. This visualization helped me silence any lingering mental vocalization. Eventually, I moved beyond the need for words or images, relying instead on the essence of the mantra—its meaning and energy—without form.

One morning, after a week of feeling slightly disconnected from my practice, I dedicated time to a prolonged meditation session (seated in my usual position, in front of my couch). I approached it without expectations, aiming only to find a steady rhythm. When the session ended, I realized something astounding had happened: *presence had now become effortless.*

There was no mental time, no thoughts, no negativity, no suffering—only calm action and peace. I navigated daily tasks with clarity, unencumbered by reactivity and mental noise. This realization marked the endpoint in my practice as it was. The mantra, the observations, and the surrender had all served their purpose, leading me to a state of pure being.

Transcending Nature

At the heart of this practice is the transcendence of fear. Fear is nature's primal force, binding us to cycles of survival and attachments. Animals live fully immersed in these cycles, acting and reacting without the self-awareness to rise beyond them. The human, however, possesses the unique ability to transcend fear into spirit through the mind and in knowledge of self. We revolt against fear by dismantling the mind's self-induced fear, desire, and attachment.

This transcendence is not about rejecting nature but about moving beyond its limitations. The mind is the bridge that leads to conscious realization. To transcend both nature and man is to embody what Nietzsche called the Übermensch (superman), the Buddha described as enlightenment, Vedanta names Sat-Chit-Ananda (absolute existence, consciousness, bliss), and Jesus referred to as the reunion with God (to be whole again). It's the ultimate reconciliation: reason and faith, mind and spirit. True alignment arises when we balance these forces, avoiding both religious fanaticism and over-rationalization. In this harmony, suffering dissolves, and we experience the Absolute, where neither fear nor doubt holds sway.

Faith and Spirit

Faith is not the blind belief in a deity or the promise of an afterlife, nor is it confined to the stories and dogmas of religion. Genuine spiritual faith is faith in the present moment, and in yourself as you are at your essence. It's a deep trust in your ability to connect with the unifying energy that flows through you and from you. This faith transcends labels and systems, pointing to the root of existence itself. Above all, it's simply faith that you're not your conditioned mind.

Different spiritual paths, whether through the Christian concept of the "Kingdom within" or the dharmic teachings of the East, and all else, ultimately converge on the same truth. Knowing yourself as something more requires more than observing metaphor, memorizing scripture, or following rituals; it requires profound self-inquiry, surrender, and practice. It's about recognizing life not as its countless extensions, but as its singular, unified source. It's what gives rise to courage, clarity, and presence. Belief built on external constructs—whether materialist or religious—can easily become distorted by the ego, leading to fanaticism, manipulation, and extreme desperation.

When misunderstood, belief binds us to mental fear, but when realized in its pure form, it becomes the antidote to fear. It allows us to approach the unknown not with dread but with curiosity and wonder. Just as fear warns of dangers hiding behind the stones in our path, faith whispers of greatness and treasures to be found beyond. It inspires us to move forward, to embrace the horizon where earth meets sky, transcending the conditions laid before us.

Have boundless faith in the words "I am." It takes a clean mind, one that is free from serving the ego, with knowledge of what you are in surrender. In this, you can touch consciousness at its source. It's the complete individual who realizes they're this source, they're the creator of reason, and that life is more than wants and fears, but something to be grateful for— "I am God. I am creative. And I am grateful."

When you embody these words, you step into your authenticity, becoming the individual who knows they are more than thoughts, negative emotions, and attachment. You're the light that shines through it all, the consciousness that witnesses and creates simultaneously. Life ceases to be something to endure or overcome; it becomes something to celebrate, something to be grateful for in every moment.

Faith in "I am" transforms existence. It clears away desperation and replaces it with a deep, abiding peace. It shifts the narrative from one of survival to one of creation and joy. And in this state of faith, of grace, gratitude flows naturally—an acknowledgment of the gift of being, the divine simplicity of presence itself.

Will From Despair

Despair is the ego's inevitable response to its limitations. It's this desperation that requires overcompensations, constant augmenting, and quenching. Unlike the term 'suffering,' which can be mistaken for something external and circumstantial, desperation is more tied to the ego's looming condition, rooted in the mind's grasping and inability to find fulfillment. It becomes our nature because we are trapped in cycles of overextended fear and attachment, bound by the ego's endless desires and aversions.

If life is generally the pursuit of desires or a search for power, this leads to the reality that all is desperation. Greed is only defined by the motivational quality to quench this desperation (desperation plus motivation equals greed). When greed loses the ability to acquire or sustain what it once craved, and the motivation is lost, we refer to this as apathy in its various forms. In general, there will always be this anticipation, or sooner or later a lack of luster, and it is this that will rule the ego-driven life. Whether we call it apathy or greed, the mother of both, at its root, is grasping, desperation.

Even when negative emotions are not overt, a life driven by egoic impulses is one of subtle, automated discontent. Despair may not always be consciously felt, but it underpins the ego's relentless and desperate striving. Degrees of despair may vary, but the root is the same—a separation from the wholeness of your singular self. In moments of pure joy or surrender, despair seems absent. This contrast gives a hint at what desperation really is: the weight of the ego, the absence of alignment with the universal self, with spirit.

Yet this suffering is not without purpose. It serves as the necessary darkness that makes the light of faith all the more evident. Faith and despair exist in a dynamic interplay, each giving meaning to the other. Without desperation, faith would lack depth and significance; without faith, desperation would lead only to collapse. It's within this tension that the human will arises—a will born not merely from survival or power, but from the yearning to transcend suffering and find peace. Whatever the result may be, the will is always, in essence, a *will from despair*.

In nature, the will can be seen as a manifestation of dominance or control, an ultimate mechanism for survival. But in humanity, it contains something more: a yearning for meaning and transcendence, precisely in contrast to the ego and its despairing duality. This is what it means to be an ape of apathy.

Even the pursuits of power, status, or success can still be seen simply as an attempt to desperately escape desperation (but never fulfilling this duty because of self-ignorance). While it's important to accept these drives as part of our human nature, the deeper will is not about manipulating the external world to achieve fleeting satisfaction. It's about aligning with the internal light of consciousness. This is the will that moves toward truth—the *will to spirit*.

Materialist perspectives strive to reduce, if not eliminate, the human will to mechanical processes: neurons firing, hormones surging, ancestral and present relationships, and so on. While these are undeniable aspects of our existence, but what do they, together, *drive* toward? When we quiet the mind and release egoic attachments, we encounter a space of freedom, malleability, and clarity, revealing that consciousness is more than the mechanical; it is meaning itself. Whether or not this realization constitutes something like "free will" is less important than the *experience* of liberation it offers—liberation of the despairing mind.

While rationality is a powerful tool, it only operates on the surface. It dissects, categorizes, and organizes, but it cannot alone reach the depths inward where the highest, most consistent form of joy, where spirit, resides—as long as it is bound up in itself. Yet, it's through reason and the rational gift of language that we have the means to reach deeper. The words "I am" are the bridge—a mantra that speaks to the root of existence, calling forth the creative force within. It's the ultimate affirmation of being, and through it, we align with the truth of who we are.

This book points to the self as spirit. Just as the unconscious (as Carl Jung suggests) reveals itself in dreams and archetypes, and every creation worth seeing or hearing emerges from a deeper, unseen source; the self as spirit holds the wellspring of all meaning. The practice of "I am" is a call to bring this unconscious source into conscious recognition. It's the act of speaking truth into existence, bearing witness to your essence. With these words, allow the ego to completely absorb into the infinite.

Liberty and the Individual

True and pure liberty is the mind's yearning for freedom, not freedom (and slavery) of the ego to indulge every passing desire, but the independence to transcend the constraints of the ego and desperation. This is the liberty of mind with spirit: the ability to move beyond unnecessary fears and attachment, aligning with the deeper truth of existence.

The *will from despair*—when channeled toward self-harmony—becomes the liberation of self. It's the act of releasing the ego's grasp, stepping out of the stress and longing that binds us. In this liberation, we come to know ourselves not as the struggling ego, but as the expansive spirit, fully capable of true freedom and natural morality.

Turning inward and looking back toward the heart is the direct path toward ease of virtue. Authentic and quiet wisdom naturally gives rise to goodness, an outcome that aligns with being connected to your core. When virtue is ignored or distorted, suffering and despair intensify. This misalignment too easily manifests as self-hatred, or a confused narcissism that denies the need for ethical connection.

Overemphasizing external laws alone—whether expressed through ancient decrees on mythical stone tablets or through the prevailing philosophies of the time—without recognizing the liberty of mind and the freedom for self-discovery, stifles the individual's journey. Genuine morality stems from within, arising from empathy grounded in self-awareness and a connection to the greater whole. By aligning with the words 'I am,' we honor the spiritual path of each individual, recognizing that true liberty comes from within, not as an external force imposed upon us, but as the natural outflow of attention and self-awareness with an authentic connection. At some point in life, everyone should strive to know themselves directly as spirit, or at the very least, explore this possibility.

The absence of spirit (or no-self) in both religious and secular ideologies can often lead to extremes. Blind fanaticism clings to resentments and rituals, while over-rationalization denies the inspirations of human experience. Both paths, when unbalanced, fail to honor the singularity of existence. Whether atheist or religious, what matters is how much you care to live, and you treat others as if they're not the egoic self, but as an Absolute one (whether concluded by determinism or a deity). The solution lies in integrating faith and reason, recognizing that they share a common goal: unity and wholeness.

When the ego's hold loosens, the spirit emerges, showing a profound sense of freedom that transcends circumstance. The words "I am" reflect this liberation, affirming the self as an individual expression of the whole, connected yet uniquely free. To practice "I am" is to embody this freedom fully, stepping into the truth of who you are beyond that which despairs.

To be Graced

The culmination of faith, surrender, and presence, when held fast and true, gives us grace—the inexhaustible, undeniable experience of spirit flowing through you. Grace is not something you can force or achieve; it's a gift that arises after pure acceptance, when the ego is quieted, and the heart is opened. It relates to those consistently emphasized terms, bliss and gratitude, which are expressions of flowing graciousness from faith.

Through grace, you feel the roots of life stretching anchored to your heart and the breath of existence moving through and from your being. Temptation holds no sway here. It's in accordance with the state of effortless alignment, where the past and future are dissolved, leaving only the present. Grace shows you that life is more than survival and manipulation; it's an expression of spirit, a dance of energy aware of itself.

When you encounter grace, follow it. Let it guide you into the depths of presence and the fullness of your being. Grace will show you the path, because it is one with the destination. It is the living embodiment of 'I am,' the full realization of spirit flowing effortlessly in life. In grace, we remember that our truest essence has always been there, waiting for us to return.

Faith, despair, virtue, liberty, and grace are all aspects of the human journey toward spirit. Each reveals a facet of greater truth: that within each of us lies the ability to transcend the ego, align with the Absolute, and live in harmony with ourselves in the world. Through surrender, presence, and the affirmation "I am," we can move beyond the cycles of grasping at what is fleeting, into the freedom of being.

Commitment

This practice demands a deep determination. There must be a willingness to relinquish all attachments and place the cessation of mental suffering at the forefront of your life's purpose. It's natural to occasionally forget to practice, but what matters is that you remember and resume your efforts. Dedicate yourself fully, disciplining your mind to relinquish all thoughts, whether they are happy, sad, nostalgic, anticipatory, repetitive, or traumatic. Recognize that you are awareness itself, not the narratives you tell yourself. Repeat this truth until it becomes your sole understanding, and then allow even that to dissipate.

Achieving effortless awareness doesn't require you to permanently maintain this state forever (as I've stated before), although you may find the experience profoundly desirable. Enlightenment can be like visiting a serene destination: you may stay for a while, basking in its tranquility and peace, but eventually, you may return to a more regular state of practice, usually in the name of some form of education and progress.

Whatever the case may be, trust that you have gained the tools to completely end suffering and maintain a clear, unencumbered mind. The ultimate aim of this practice is to enhance your existence. This book is not just about achieving an elevated state, but also about incorporating these practices into your everyday life at your own pace. If you do reach this heightened state of awareness, understand that you can always leave and return to it—it remains accessible and will not fade away.

Embrace your identity as the "I am" presence. Go inward, feel this energy as you speak it, and give it your full attention as it drifts down. Nothing will be more fulfilling in your life. If you encounter difficulties, take a conscious breath and engage in the practice. If there is no struggle, simply remain in stillness.

The Three Paths

There was a man who had heard, since childhood, of a great tree that gave the fruit of everlasting fulfillment. Some said the tree was only for the worthy, that to touch it before death was forbidden. Others claimed that its fruit was merely a symbol, never meant to be tasted. Many sat in the distance, drawing pictures of its beauty, and singing praises of what they had never seen. They spoke of how, one day, after suffering and death, they would finally be granted a taste, and all others would be left to suffer.

The man listened to their words, but something unsettled him. He noticed that, despite their devotion, few seemed to be nourished. Their songs were filled with longing, while their drawings were intricate yet empty. They never moved closer. The terrain was treacherous, the hill steep, and the leaves thick and tangled, keeping the fruit away and hidden from view.

He also noticed others, ones that had turned their back on the tree entirely. They see only the land before them—the cities, the people, the works of human hands—and call this the meaning, and the thoughts which helped create it the highest value. Many paint the beauty of what was created and can be seen, felt, and measured, dismissing the tree as a childish fantasy. "What fools," one of them says, shaking his head at those who sit before it. "They waste their lives waiting for something that is beyond here, clinging to stories when they could make something of their time. They fear death, so they invent eternity. How embarrassing." To them, meaning is not found in the fruit they have never seen, but in the tangible joys of material comfort and progress.

The man stood between the two groups, uncertain. He walks forward. As he passes, he admires the devotion of the believers and the artistry of the materialists, but sees their limitations. The worshipers are bound by faith without experience, and the materialists are bound by experience without faith. He doesn't argue with them or try to prove them wrong. Instead, he steps beyond them both and goes to the tree himself, makes his way through the weeds and bushes with his own hands.

As he moved nearer, climbing higher up the hill, the noise of the world behind him faded. The further he went, the clearer his vision became. The doubts, once so loud, grew quiet—not because they had been answered by logic, but because they no longer mattered.

And then, in a clearing, he saw it.

If there were a sword afire guarding the tree,

he would discover it to be an illusion. If there were a voice telling him to turn back, he would see that it was his own hesitation, not truth. He doesn't need to believe in the fruit's promise, nor does he need to reject it—he simply reaches out, takes hold of it, and tastes.

He came to understand that it was more than the fruit itself that fulfilled him, and it wasn't that the tree held any power over him. It was that he had *moved*, that he had *tasted*, that he had broken free from the illusion and denial. He followed the inkling to its end, and the fulfillment had been possible all along. The others, too, could taste it—life itself—if only they would step forward and away from their judgment.

But each had their own path, their own doubts to confront. Some would never leave their spot beyond the tree, believing themselves unworthy of the reward. Others would scoff at something they had never dared to seek in earnest.

He looked back once, then turned his gaze forward. With quiet certainty, he stepped beyond the tree, into whatever lay ahead.

Recap

Repeat a mantra instead of letting a thought continue. In this, through your strength of mind and the elimination of regret and negativity, you expedite the process of full enlightenment. My mantra was "I am God, I am creative, and above all, I am grateful" in various forms. I'll note, in this when I spoke "I am God," I would feel energy shoot to my center, and ball up and hold there; when I said the words "I am creative," I would feel my fingertips feel as though on fire with energy; and lastly, when I said "I am grateful," the energy stored at my heart and anywhere else would explode up and be released. These were my personal experiences, and while I don't claim them to be universal or overly important, they were undeniable to me. I encourage anyone to find their own words, their resonance. Still, these words capture the essence of what this book aims to convey. Use this step as a replacement for step one, though you can still do both if you want or when first starting this step.

It's crucial not to trust thoughts that seem helpful by critiquing or highlighting mistakes, particularly those with any negative connotations. These thoughts offer no real value and should be rooted out as soon as noticed, with no worth to be observed, but with the same ease as what is usual. While you might occasionally have thoughts that remind you of your practice, beware of those that provide constant, unhelpful commentary.

As you progress, you can also move beyond words toward a more peaceful state and replace the "I am" mantra with the words spelled out as in an image in your mind. I would see the letters in red with a black background toward the end of this process, as a means to help end the mantra. I cannot say for certain these are necessary, but they helped me when I needed them, and may help you too.

Embrace the identity of "I am." Feel and acknowledge this as your essential reality, and let it guide you to embody your highest self—the spirit. Let the mantra resonate deeply within you, releasing all conditioned thoughts and transforming negative energy into inner peace and appreciation. Whenever you falter, return to this practice and ground yourself in the present moment. Over time, you may reach a state of effortless awareness, where no further effort is required. Simply remain inward-focused, fully aware of your true self.

Today, as the world has evolved, I believe there is no more important question to be asked: Am I a soul? Or am I mind and body? Or nothing?

Can it be that you are something more, something untouchable by the corporeal? Something perhaps embarrassing to speak about in today's secular, grown societies? Perhaps the idea of a soul is merely a relic of past superstitions. But if so, why does it persist? Why does its presence feel undeniable in our greatest works of art, in the music that moves us, in stories that transcend time, in the quiet pull of intuition, in the awe that leaves us breathless?

If you want to find out if you have a soul, the mind must be let go; and in turn, to discover you are mind alone, you must let go of the soul. Spirituality seeks to reclaim the perfection that, in its view, was obscured by the intellect's ego. Secular ideals, on the other hand, see perfection as something to be built upon into the future, progressing until intellect alone defines human achievement. Both perspectives hold true, but individual fulfillment lies in rediscovering the self as spirit and living as spirit, allowing the finite to reach its potential through spirit's pure virtue.

MEDITATION

The "I Am" Mantra

Settle into stillness. Let your body release its weight. Let the breath slow and calm . Let the grip of the ego and the world outside loosen.

You are not rushing.
You are not reaching.
You are returning.

Breathe deep down into the body, lightly expanding in this infinite space. Let the breath move like a wave through you, arriving without force, leaving without resistance.

When you have quieted enough into stillness—when within becomes a gateway that accepts all self-suggestion and energy—then speak these first words into those depths:

"I am God."

Let the phrase fall with the sense of endlessness. Let it echo through the space within you that cannot be seen, only felt.

You are not claiming superiority.
You are not becoming something else.
You are remembering and reuniting with what you are beneath every thought, beyond every condition.
You are pure awareness.
You are presence itself.
You are the stillness that allows life to move.

Let the words drop again—*I am God*—feel the words from the heart, from this authentic you, not the mind. This is the deeper self, silent and steady; know them to be true.

Now, on your next inhale, breathe deeper into the heart.

And on the next exhale, speak inwardly:

"I am Creative."

If God is the air containing all, then creativity is your fire. The spark that moves the engine. The taker and the giver. It is inspiration, the connected individual. This is your expression—not merely what you do, but how you are.

Feel the energy travel to the fingertips...to the lips...to the chest. Wherever your gift seeks form, breathe into it. Breathe life into the fire.

On the next breath, with fullness of presence (take time to return to presence if needed), speak:

"I am Grateful."

Let the words carry weight.
Not for a list of blessings or a passing emotion—
But for existence itself.

Grateful to be aware.
Grateful to create.
Grateful for opportunities and life's lessons.

This is not the gratitude of the mind, but of the soul.
It holds joy and sorrow without resistance.
It knows everything within cause and effect,

compensation, and spirit, has brought you here, and it bows in reverence.

Now inhale again...
Let the breath fill your chest as light.

Repeat the complete mantra slowly within you:

"I am God. I am creative. And above all, I am grateful."

Let each phrase carry its own rhythm.
Let each one settle in its place in the body.
If the energy rises, let it.
If it stills, rest in this stillness.

Repeat as many times as you want. And if thoughts arise, notice them and return. There is no perfection in practice, only presence.

When you are ready to close, let the final breath be full and slow. End not with the mind but with the feeling that remains.
The words may fade,
But their truth stays with you.

You are God.
You are Creative.
You are Grateful.
And this is enough.

Do this meditation anytime during any hour of the day, whether it's a quick repetition within three breaths or longer and more focused. Whenever possible, let it be your practice.

RECAPTURING

THE ABSOLUTE

You have got to be completely honest with yourself, seeing every weakness of thought and emotion, letting what was once you shatter and be swept away. Return to this moment over and over, and over again, without question, without doubt or resistance.

See the mind as it is: the obscurer. Pause it through paradox, using time against it and questioning it, trying to imagine the next thought, anticipating an answer that will never come. Know the ego in its inauthenticity and judgment, and stop drowning in unconscious compulsion. Be indifferent to thinking and grateful in emotion.

Surrender to the Absolute. Whether you believe in determined biology or a deity, the intent should be the same: you are the universal self, or there is no self, with no difference between the two options. There can be no more middle ground, no more confusion, you're one and the same as any other, and there is nothing truer. Surrender deep into your emotions and through your inner essence. Live at the heart and breathe life into this singular presence, recognizing it as the consciousness that's been forgotten in overactivity.

See the world around you as the objective, clear observer, and in doing so, see the unity cf presence in all, the connection of one fluid moment. Hone your ability to have a singular focus, through sight, sound, and physical feelings. In a singular focus, undistracted by thoughts, you grow to know yourself as you really are. Concentrate away from concepts and know your root. In this root is ecstasy, perfect consciousness, God.

Recognize this answer as the replacement thought to all thoughts, allowing this recognition to enter the deepest recesses of your mind and body. Speak the words "I am God" until they become concrete and undeniable, and you will transform. It is God as the ethereal, mysterious, and eternal presence. Nothing more. It isn't something that thinks or judges; it's that which emits prudence, gratitude, and meaning, beyond any condition anyone can lay upon it. Tell this source, "I am grateful," every time you recognize it as you, so the ego may know its place of nonrecognition. Don't forget you're allowed to create, because you're the creator, knowing, "I am creative."

Breathe each statement deeply into your heart and let it resonate without end. Live this one realization.

There are plenty of sweet memories, surely difficult to let go of. Songs sang with friends. Babies embracing you and giving you a kind of warmth you didn't know existed. First dates, weddings, and everything in between. A dog happy to see you, a new haircut, and you even lost some weight. Mornings basked in a warm, calm glow. But there is darkness too.

Life gives you plenty of curveballs, plenty of things to be upset about, and plenty of choices that will have dire implications. There will be spectrums upon spectrums of what should have or should not have been. In the past, there will be sorrow that colors the present. In the future, possible dreams or nightmares come true. There are people who don't deserve what they have, and there is you, not getting what you deserve. There is a car that injects you with insecurity as it flies by. A woman or a man who makes you feel small at a glance. There is hatred, resentment, guilt, and depression. You will be motivated, then you won't. You'll grow older and become a bit calmer. You'll grow even older and have no sense of identity. A political view annoys you. Egalitarian? Hierarchical?

The difference? Conquer fear in death alone.

But how shall I die? When shall I die? Is there meaning in death?

The secret is that every thought wishes it was found out and dissipated into nothingness. Your mind longs to be unraveled and turned silent. Despair looms with constant numbness over it, and it goes unnoticed because it has become your way of being. Here is true and pure liberty: the ego faltering and committing suicide, and leaving nothing behind to suffer over. Its clinch is tight and a headache, and medication in any form might just allow it to die for a moment, but it will never compare to ego's sweet and complete death.

And somewhere within life beckons. It shows itself in all things worthwhile, hoping to be seen, begging to be rediscovered. It wants all the pendulums to be dropped and the moment to be accepted. It yearns to life as it was when eyes first opened, where the original and all-encompassing dependence was a gift from your mother's embrace, before consciousness was covered by make-believe and fear. It's in the lessons of great stories and gives appeal to a thing like faith in return for the desperation of personal good, over personal evil. Something wants to live, wants to thrive over surviving, and it thrives in deep silence.

Will you walk that sacred path of mental silence? Caring for each breath, letting go of what has been most consistent for so long, devoting yourself to something unprovable outside of personal experience? Perhaps your mind is just stronger than mine, than others who have gone down similar roads, and your mind refuses to give itself up despite its suffering. Maybe you don't see what the big deal is? And whether you suffer or not, you are doing just fine. But have no doubt—ego requires comfort, and comfort in great lands of progress requires great desperation and manipulation, only augmented by reprieves of gracious faith.

For fruition, that faith has to be real in sacrifice. Faith that this ego is not me, no matter how convincing the fantasy. Faith that the great inkling is not a biological lie, some archaic fib to keep you from walking off a cliff. But this faith, in full, requires pride, pity, friends, family, to be given up as having any priority or purpose above the Absolute. Whether this is a conscious understanding or an unconscious understanding through suffering, it's to be accepted.

You go alone, into the eternal glory of returning perfection within. Treat the path with reverence, for only in solitude can the ego be completely crushed. Not physical isolation, but in the nature of your existence. Nearly always, as seen in psychology and spirituality, the weakness of the ego's infatuated vanity in the approval and acceptance from others gives us our awakening moments. These attachments will eventually reveal their uselessness. While in the midst of your spiritual endeavor, hold off on explaining the great things you learn and your desire to share them; for now, they are yours, and opinions are meaningless. Think of it this way: your consciousness is a sacred artifact; if you start sharing it, someone might just steal it away. Hold it close, selfishly, protect it.

But what of that special bond with a loved one? Just ask ol' Adam—he might say the real original sin was codependency. So, the loved one gets lumped into the pile with the rest to be let go, not in bitterness, but in respect for the human soul. It's only the ego, in expectation and grandiosity, that clings. All is gifted by the moment, and in this is virtue: where principles are held at the everlasting, prudential heart, and emotions are delegated as the weather of the brain's conceptions. Love. And love furiously! But love in complete presence alone, and watch smiles arise. In this, you open the possibility for what you've discovered to be discovered by others through you, without manipulation.

You can think of your life like a car, with only

so much allocated funds to maintain it. If all your resources are directed to the exterior—how others perceive you—the interior will decay. The transmission slips, the engine knocks, but you save your last dimes to buff out a scratch on the bumper and install a loud exhaust. Who cares if you're uncomfortable behind the wheel, if the car shakes and rattles—what matters is that others feel what you feel about what they see, as you momentarily drive by.

Most of these are people you don't even know. If you did, you'd keep your distance anyway—just in case they get a peek inside. So maybe it's time to do some cleaning. Put value back into you—what makes you uncomfortable, what isn't based on the fleeting considerations of others. Clean out your mind and breathe from that presence through your feelings— then get back on the road, on a path worth taking.

As it is, the path is yours—nothing can or should change that. Use the tools in whatever rhythm or combination serves you best, at whatever pace feels right. Watch your surroundings in all their beauty. Listen intently to both the silence and the noise. Go inward whenever you find yourself drifting from the moment. Use conscious breathing to aid relaxation, and feel your hands and feet and fully engage your senses. Whenever compelled, speak your "I am" message internally. Remember, you are awareness. Maintain a quiet mind.

The point of this practice is not perfection, but fulfillment without condition. Whether you use all the tools or just one, let what works best for you guide your path. Don't stress over shortcomings or specific milestones; stay honest, stay disciplined, and trust your path to unfold in its own way. In this, there is no failure.

Let wisdom support your practice. Use the mind on itself and rise above thought's compulsions. Recognize that every personality is only a mask, and underneath them all is the same essence—awareness. These masks are, too, just manifestations of the one root consciousness.

Clinging to what brings pleasure inevitably leads to dissatisfaction and pain, and back again. The trap of this cycle holds the appeal of returning to your true self, the self that resides at the heart and has no opposite: the Absolute. This inherent, often hidden radiance that we all possess never changes and never departs. Surrendering to the Absolute ends the cycle of intense emotional swings, repetitive negativity, and compulsive reactions spurred by mental fear and dependence.

Dependency isn't evil; it's motivation is the love for wholeness. But when external needs become the source of identity, disappointment follows. Let go of judgment and control and let the heart return to appreciation. Suffering comes from forgetting liberation is possible—from believing we are our thoughts and their demands. But we are not bound by the mind's story. Let go of conditions. Let love replace judgment. Open fully, and the world opens too.

You might have noticed a common theme through every step, which is to be what is called "one-pointed." Whether watching thoughts, sensing within, observing the world, or affirming the "I am," there is consistent practice of unburdened focus. In time, these styles of presence converge. Mental noise softens, and clarity emerges. Every moment is its own, so respond naturally. Sometimes a breath will center you. Sometimes, quiet observation will do. Trust what arises.

Treat every thought or reaction equally—none more important or shameful than another. You're not these mental ripples; you're the stillness beneath them. When a reaction comes, acknowledge it, accept it, and let it go. If you miss the moment, begin again. Always be releasing. Let yourself be the kind of person who learns from mistakes and moves forward, without being defined by them.

This is not arrogance—it's humility through presence. If others question your detachment, you might just say, "I care, but I've chosen not to dwell. That's how I grow." Or, just go on your merry way. To be identified with every thought or emotion is to live in reaction. But peace comes from returning to awareness—again and again—until even the pull of emotionally charged thoughts quickly dissolves. In this way, we can fully surrender to what is within.

Positivity and Growth

Never underestimate a cheerful disposition. No conversation can feel more divine than one that begins with "excuse me, my apologies," then is replied to with "it's okay," and is accompanied by a smile—there is power in a smile. When we stay true to ourselves, embracing our distinctions with an everlasting inward presence, a joyful feeling is impossible to deny.

There are individuals out there, of the opinion that decent conduct and general respect, and apologies too, are somehow only related to the fawning of lesser animals in nature—but in this opinion, you see how far the ego can stray from the truth of our nature.

After all, what can show more vitality, more keenness toward thriving than the willingness to show you care about life? Not to show in an over-empathetic and overly modest way, but in such a way that the care you exude honors life itself; in a way that proves not only respect toward others, but the value you hold toward yourself.

Generally, what we want is to feel good and not think so much. You can feel good on command, on average, and the more you practice it, the easier it becomes. The more negativity is drained, the stronger the positivity can grow. The mind can be the tricky part, eliminating this comes with a constant growing meditative habit. Another thing to remember is that ridding yourself of one vein of negative emotion is worth a thousand negative thoughts.

The more you engage in these practices and the longer you can maintain this focused state, the more proficient you become, and the easier it gets. Strive to extend your periods of presence each day, gradually increasing your effort. Meditate as often as possible and have a meditative way of being in everyday life moments. This commitment—starting each day ready to resume your practice and ending it on a strong note—is where true growth happens. Let mental strength and an appreciation for silence become routine. While some may find this simplicity boring, embrace these moments as opportunities for greatness, where your true purpose can unfold.

There will be days and even years when breaks seem in short supply. I'll note that during the apex of my personal growth in presence, although I was working ten or more hour shifts about six days a week, I was limited in my daily social duties. I had a lot of time to myself, and having discovered that I have a say in what thoughts come in, and having grown weary of consistent suffering, the recipe was there.

What I learned was to take time to be present and to turn those everyday habitual moments into times of practice. Even if some bodily action is involved, use the opportunity and grow stronger. You may have a family, or a volatile relationship, hate filled people to deal with at a job, a career that requires your full attention to be successful, an absorptive fork in the road of life—whatever the challenge is, work to create the space when you can, and know this space and practice will help overcome any obstacle in your path. There may be a day when you have nothing but time, remember the choice you have, and take back control.

Who is the Absolute?

The Absolute perceives the spirit in everyone and everything, free from prejudice or judgment. They see themselves as equals to all, neither superior nor inferior to anybody. This equality eliminates animosity and fosters harmonious interactions with others. While individuals may serve as inspirations or teachers, evoking natural appreciation, the tendency to over-glamorize is diminished. Such balance garners respect and cultivates lighthearted, comfortable conversations, as well as an inexhaustible respect that extends beyond mere control through fear.

Moreover, the Absolute is immune to manipulation. Armed with a deep understanding of the ego, they recognize attempts at manipulation as sources of suffering and can readily identify such tactics. This awareness also negates any desire to manipulate others. Instead of drawing others into their sphere with expectations, they radiate reality and attract others through genuine actions and intent. Striving for external validation is seen as unnecessary. True to their nature, the Absolute engages in interactions that are rooted in sincerity and mutual respect, understanding that force meets resistance, if not sooner, then later.

It's not only in others that the Absolute is recognized, but also in all surroundings, objects, and space. For the Absolute, everything is part of a unified whole, a flowing moment of fullness. When awareness is pure and focused, all that receives attention merges into a single entity. This results in a constant flow of peace and joy, though spiritual energy and sensory perceptions may fluctuate. The consistent pursuit is awareness in the moment, internally and externally.

Though the Absolute is all-encompassing, there is an objective awareness of the individual that can see all separate objects as if they were only for observation. There is no confusion through labels and distracting thoughts. Pure sight, sound, and feel exist with, and without, both the space and material of all. What is invisible is seen. What is silent is heard. What is unfelt is felt. When knowledge of the one self is found, these things become possible.

In the state of the Absolute, there is no required result or anticipation. Thoughts, being constructs confined within time, hold no sway here. The Absolute doesn't harbor expectations, positive or negative, nor dwells on past experiences. Any past dramatization is seen for its limitations and the obstacles it creates. While worldly knowledge may be necessary for a comfortable life—unless one chooses a path of spiritual solitude—the conditioning from the past was essential for societal interaction, but must be transcended into a continual moment of deep awareness.

What remains is merely the shell of the ego. The Absolute uses its developed character as a guide, elevating others without hesitation, embodying the virtues it has given over to. The dismissal of the ego and the proclamation that "no personality resides here" are viewed as trivial, possibly even as remnants of a latent ego. Such statements can introduce unnecessary drama, often muddying the clarity of spiritual communication.

Whether deeply engaged in practice or having attained enlightenment, there's no need for boasting about such states as if they were accomplishments. The once all-encompassing personality, a source of much suffering, is now completely diminished or perhaps utilized selectively, having been integrated into one.

The Absolute moves with a calm demeanor and perfect timing, unaffected by the rush of time. This embodies balance and acts according to what naturally should be done. Their actions are not characterized by passivity (although that can be appropriate in certain situations) but by a willingness to let things unfold naturally. Activity might lessen, especially toward those driven by ego or in conditions that have lost their appeal. Still, the Absolute always considers and demonstrates right action when interacting with people and pursuing goals, uninfluenced by opinions. Though there is a gentle hand, there is perfectly timed aggression, because there could be nothing otherwise in a world devoid of regret. No thought, whether from themselves or others, causes significant distraction. The Absolute sees through superficiality and remains unmoved by another's dissatisfaction or fluctuating emotions.

This equanimity comes from a learned ability to avoid getting entangled in drama or excessive internal dialogue. Understanding that others may be trapped in such cycles, the Absolute neither blames nor dismisses them. Instead, they offer their complete presence, freely given yet not demanding acceptance. If engagement is chosen, patience and acceptance are shown, allowing situations to evolve naturally without personal attachment, benefiting everyone involved.

The Absolute is generous but not naive. They give unconditionally, without expectations, yet not without an awareness of the situation. Focused attention is often the greatest gift they offer. If physical sustenance is needed, it is provided judiciously; if inner joy is sought, it may radiate from them naturally as a gift to be accepted or unaccepted. Ultimately, the Absolute freely offers whatever they can afford to give.

Practices like fasting, chastity, and other forms of asceticism may benefit those still tormented by self-judgment and somewhat influenced by the opinions of others; however, for those truly on the Absolute path, these measures are unnecessary. Through consistent practice and the release of attachments, self-judgment fades, virtues emerge naturally, and the struggle with compulsive thinking and negative thoughts diminishes. While some might choose asceticism, either intentionally or inadvertently, the ultimate guidance should always prioritize surrender and presence.

At the start of their spiritual journey, many find concepts like embracing "stillness within" or engaging in meditation mundane. Yet, those who strive to reach the state of the Absolute quickly learn to cherish these practices. This appreciation may initially serve as a means to deepen presence, but can also evolve into a pursuit of broader knowledge. This could extend beyond spiritual teachings to include gaining insights into finance, investing, sales, or discovering and pursuing a new, more fulfilling career path.

It's important to note that transformation is not always instantaneous—it can take years—and the outcome may not align with initial expectations. Not all who embark on a spiritual path become recluses; some may even become authors. Regardless of whether an external passion is kindled, the primary commitment remains to spirituality and maintaining a mental state focused on the process rather than the outcome.

The Absolute bends with the wind but never breaks, embodying versatility. They see themselves reflected in others, leading with respect, appreciation, and empowerment. They create leaders, follow attentively, and embrace without overwhelming. For them, life flows in its natural progression—there is no fear of dreams turning into nightmares, only a steady, balanced reality.

The Absolute is Dharma, the Tao, Atman, the Holy Spirit. It dwells at the core of being and expresses itself through focused awareness. Countless stories and proverbs throughout the ages urge us to shift our focus from the head to the heart. This shift is crucial because the mind is a breeding ground for unnatural problems: it fragments reality until nothing remains, over-intellectualizes survival to the point where fear dominates our lives, leading us into cycles of tiredness, depression, apprehension, anger, and apathy.

To reside in awareness at the heart is to reject the cyclical and impermanent nature of conditioned thoughts that construct the ego. It's a commitment to steadfast wellbeing and offering undivided attention without deviation.

Ending

We can simply view our bodies as composed of the elements that sustain life: earth, water, air, and fire. The earth gives birth to the body and absorbs it back in death. It's the stone that rolls or gathers moss, a blatant and solid reality, a connection that restricts and gives life. Water travels through the veins of mountains and men alike, to the oceans and evaporates into the atmosphere and back; it's change, and it's the flow of life. Air—the space that holds everything together while being nothingness—is all, and it is nothing; it is mystery, it contains and is one with the soul. Like the sun, fire is a relentless energy, inspiration, and invention; it pushes life forward, yet it also destroys it, just as oxygen fills our lungs and decays flesh. This fire is power.

The death of the body is only a part of the elemental cycle, a cessation of the temporary life that these elements nurture. Movement proliferates and then decays back to the soil; water evaporates into the ether; molecules combust and are recycled by gravity's pull. While I'm no scientist or physicist, I see this all as in relation to the cyclical nature of stars and cosmic matter.

As for rebirth, it represents what is left behind in the quest for bliss—the endless cycle of being washed away and reborn, consumed by fire and cooled in infinite repetition. To overlook the impermanence of life and the constant dissatisfaction of a constructed mindset, and to remain devoted to the mental game, is to embrace an eternal rotation of suffering.

Those trapped in the cycle of rebirth are essentially experiencing the relentless crashes of an ego. It's part of being deeply entwined in the world. Developing a sense of personhood is necessary since we live in a society that has moved beyond mere survival. Yet, part of spiritual growth involves what might be called a "reversal stage," or realization. Although we shape our identities through mental observation and sensory experiences, there should ideally come a moment in everyone's life when the path of spirituality is embraced.

To be truly effective, spirituality must be approached as an honest endeavor. While some may become entangled in mysticism, elaborate rituals, or practices driven by selfish motives, the essence of spirituality lies in objective reason and inner calm. Others may fixate on church dogmas, which might benefit some but can also foster feelings of division and unnecessary fear. Then some engage with spirituality solely through intellectual means, using it as a problem to be solved without ever truly experiencing it. True spirituality requires active practice and experience, not just talk or show.

While acceptance is a valuable perspective, initiating spiritual growth does require a form of non-acceptance of old conditionings and the imposed notions of self. You must be sick of being sick. Hate that you hate. Be hurt that you hurt and can be hurt. Be upset that you're so weak you can be overwhelmed. Only then can you delve within and let these burdens fall away. Recognize the conditioning for what it is and realize you have a choice. Learn the practices that reverse the repression of emotions and develop a mind that only thinks constructively.

Know that there exists only one moment, shared across the vastness of the universe, from the furthest speck to everything in between. The ultimate freedom comes from living in this moment, unburdened by worries of outcomes. Learn to distinguish between your personality and your true self, see the seasons of life clearly, and discern what needs to be kept and what should be released. If you dwell in time, it will master you; if you live beyond time, you will master it.

With every conscious breath, release your attachments. Let go of clinging to anger, pain, pleasure, purity, perfection, concepts of right and wrong, resentment, infatuation, aversion, intrigue, elation, status, pride, and all other shifting and fleeting illusions. The attempt to manipulate your mental state by grasping at people and things can be resolved once you recognize that fulfillment and inner peace are your root states. Bliss is termed such only because it is obstructed; without these obstructions, it would simply be your being. Every desire is essentially a yearning to return to this blissful state, and the act of grasping is an incorrect approach prompted by misguided mental processes.

Conceptual fears and the suffering they cause will diminish with dedicated practice. If you find yourself struggling, the ultimate advice is to let go.

Whether you're an artist mastering your craft, an employee in a job you despise seeking purpose, a new millionaire grappling with unease, or if you find yourself homeless, letting go is the first step toward liberation.

Letting go, surrender, and acceptance are all facets of the same gem—they are spirituality. Whether through this practice or that, any method that resonates with truth is worthwhile. There's no habit as fulfilling or as devoid of adverse effects as plain and pure spirituality. Let go of negative and compulsive thoughts, surrender your emotions, accept peace, and observe nature. These are the foundational principles of this book, accompanied by detailed steps to guide you. Cast aside doubt, and perceive concepts for what they truly are. If questions arise, delve deeply and view your thoughts objectively as separate events, and simply observe the origin of your thoughts.

It's essential to meditate (purposefully, in solitude) at least once a day, and more if possible. Whether it's for twenty minutes, ten minutes, five minutes, or even ten seconds, any amount of time spent meditating is beneficial. Whatever time you have, take pride in the effort made. If you find it challenging to deepen your meditation, begin by simply observing your surroundings without attaching labels. If intrusive thoughts persist, shift your focus from negativity to increasingly positive thoughts, perhaps using a positive mantra to guide your practice. Remember, positivity poses fewer obstacles than negativity and brings numerous benefits. After that, you can use the Step One technique of *paradoxical intention,* and watch your mind expecting another thought to arise, and wait there. Alternatively, simply focus on your breath; remember, there's no such thing as a bad meditation. The most important thing is to show up.

It's counterproductive to succumb to the overthinker within and adopt a mindset of helplessness or self-criticism, such as saying, "I can't control it, people don't understand," or "there's just something wrong with me." While it may be tempting to seek validation from friends who might tell you what you want to hear, this can inadvertently reinforce negative self-perceptions. Others may even think of you privately in terms like "narcissist" and "destructive behavior." Some may indeed struggle more than others due to inherent tendencies, but spiritual practice is achievable for everyone, regardless of the starting point. For many, the problem is straightforward: too much negative thinking (usually about what other people think). This often manifests as egotism or self-destructive behavior, driven by a need to manipulate one's environment and the people in it to satisfy mental conditions like self-pity, anger, apathy, pride, or guilt and shame. Ultimately, this leads to suffering.

Accepting a life dominated by substance abuse, depression, anxiety, suicidal tendencies, and simmering hatred is a waste of potential. If excessive negative thinking is your struggle, then it's crucial to find ways to pause this cycle and create a more cheerful disposition. Achieving a breakthrough doesn't necessarily require an epiphany or a sudden surge in self-confidence, though these may occur—the solution has always been the same for anyone facing chronic addiction or enduring suffering: surrender. For some, intense suffering may make this solution immediately apparent, while others might need to engage in a bit more soul-searching. The extent of your suffering and your predisposition toward mindfulness will likely determine the time and effort required; however, it's accessible to all, and the level of grace given to anyone at any time is unpredictable.

The effort is your own. I can describe what effort might look like and guide you toward it, but I cannot make you exert it. It involves a commitment to study, implementing practices, and taking the correct actions. While mindfulness may seem non-active—emphasizing letting go—it initially requires a proactive engagement or a gentle pulling effort. If 'effort' feels like a paradox, consider it learning to gradually relax your grip.

Armed with the mental clarity that mindfulness provides, any goals pursued are more likely to be realized. Mindfulness teaches us to find fulfillment in the present moment, easing the burden of any action and clarifying its appropriateness. It promotes a positive outlook and attitude; remember, nothing impacts the trajectory of your life as significantly as freeing yourself from negative and obsessive thoughts and emotions. Give over to a positive attitude, and you are poised to manifest a life truly worth living.

Within us resides something constant, unbound by past or future, a source of endless satisfaction that defies complete description. Whether there is a divinity that assigns souls to each new body from above, or something dwelling in an underworld which judges our morality, remains beyond my knowing. Yet, something profound exists within us—accessible once barriers fall away, feeling deeply natural. If there is a heaven, it's this state; if there is a hell, it's living lost in and as the mind.

Adam and Eve erred in eating from the tree of the knowledge of good and evil, while the tree of life remained safeguarded, indicating that the mistake lies in the invention of good and evil, not bad itself. Krishna counseled Arjuna not on the dichotomy of right and wrong, but on the importance of surrendering both the sense of doership and attachment to outcomes. Buddha taught that our suffering stems from identifying too closely with the mind, advising detachment. Similarly, Jesus did not speak of a celestial palace above but pointed to a timeless realm within.

The purest spiritual teachings identify an overly anticipatory mind as a fundamental flaw, while suggesting that the essence of divinity—or our higher self—resides within us, here and now. If a theistic perspective does not resonate with you, consider this essence as your higher self, ever-present and waiting to be acknowledged. No grand revelations are necessary; simply recognize when you are in its presence and remain there.

It's not hidden in the stars above or buried deep in the ground, but sits within each of us, gently pulsing with the rhythm of our heart and breath. Peace, joy, and understanding do not come from the world around us—they bloom from within. Every moment of practice is a step closer to this inner sanctuary, a place where every breath is the essence of the universe and every moment is an eternity. Carry this wisdom in your heart, and let it guide you through your life, illuminating your path with the enduring light of your spirit. Be fulfilled without requirement. Take the Absolute Path.

"The greatest hazard of all, losing the self, can occur very quietly in the world, as if it were nothing at all."

—Søren Kierkegaard

The Sickness Unto Death

FINAL MEDITATION

The Practice of Undying Gratitude

Begin by settling. Sit or lie down. Let your breath arrive as it is. Let your body be precisely where it is. Allow stillness to take root within.

Imagine what undying gratitude feels like.
Not the kind that arises from listing your blessings, but something deeper. Something primal. A still, expansive thankfulness that bypasses thought entirely and trembles with the weight of what's been given.

To touch it, imagine this:
You're standing with your family—your partner, children, those whose lives are knotted into yours. For some reason beyond your control, you're moments from death in front of them.

A soldier, a man trained to see you as an enemy, raises his weapon. There's no way out.

But then, someone steps forward. A man you barely know, or maybe don't know at all. And he offers himself.
He says, "Take me instead."
For whatever reason, the offer is accepted. He dies.
You live.
You and your family walk away, carrying your life forward in the space where his ended.

Now—feel that.
Feel the gratitude that would erupt from that moment, not just light, but heavy. Not sweet, but aching.
It's the kind of gratitude that humbles you into silence.
The kind that aches with reverence because it knows the cost.
Because it contains a darkness you cannot deny—a brush against finality, a witness to sacrifice—and yet, somehow, it doesn't collapse under the weight.
Instead, it shines more clearly because of it.

This is the seed.
Let it settle inward.

Take a breath slower than usual.
Breathe that gratitude to the core of your being.
At the bottom of your exhale, linger. Rest there.
Let the feeling settle into the quiet, into the stillness.

On the next inhale, imagine you're receiving rejuvenated spirit. (Its okay to take more breaths than pointed out while reading, just follow naturally)
At the top of breath, become the witness, basking in that spirit.
Observe your mind gently, like you're standing at a distance, watching a quiet sky, waiting to see what thought appears.

Exhale again, surrendering.
Let go back into the gratefulness.

Inhale again—this time listen.
Open your hearing as if you were behind a closed door, trying to catch the smallest details.
Let sound wash over you.
Then, hear the silence between the sounds. Let that silence be part of you.

Repeat an exhale of gratitude.

Inhale again, now look.
See what surrounds you without labeling it.
Let your gaze be clear, like it's closing in on each form.
Then soften your focus. See the space that holds the form.
See not just the thing, but its place in the whole.

Now close your eyes for a moment into the moment.
Sense the energy within your hands...your chest... your face.
Or perhaps the whole body at once.
Then ask, with complete sincerity and stillness:
What is it that is sensing this?

If the practice is flowing and you feel steady in it, accept what you truly are.
On the next exhale, while feeling that undying gratitude, speak inwardly:

"I am God."

Not as the mind that judges.
But as the inner light.
Utterly individual. Completely unified with all.

This is the practice of surrender.

Do it every time you realize you're not doing it.
Do it more each day.
And if you fall away from it, that's okay.
The next moment is a perfect place to begin again.

When the moment brings with it sorrow, fear, or anger, let that become the focus instead.
Don't run from it.
Breathe with it. Let it rise in its fullness.
Accept it completely.
Let it intensify—not as pain, but as energy being reclaimed.

You will move through emotional turmoil with less friction.
You will begin to recover more quickly.
You will react less and feel more.

Because when you're no longer afraid to be wrong, to feel, to have faith,
You're free to let go.

About the Author

E. J. Albert is a father and spiritual writer whose life revolves around the guiding principle of presence, and a quiet commitment to spirituality. While he spends much of his time immersed in creative work, his deepest fulfillment comes from time with his family. He credits the path described in this book as the foundation not only of his work, but of his entire way of being. Everything he does revolves around his relationship within.

Though he has only minimal college experience and has worked a range of entry level jobs, including a few supervisory roles, he values that time for what it taught him. It offered a real-life grounded understanding of people and the dynamics of the everyday world—an education he finds worthwhile and respectable.

He intends to continue exploring consciousness and its relationship to ego for as long as he lives. While he makes no claims to originality or the discovery of ultimate answers, he remains committed to one thing: doing his part to live as an authentic human being.

Thank you for reading.

May this book be a reminder of *who*, and *where,* you are. The quietness within.

—E. J. Albert

To connect or learn more:
www.ejalbert.com
contact@ejalbert.com